GLEANINGS
FROM
A DUFF HOUSE GARDENER'S DIARY

Banff 1873-4

Gleanings: things, especially facts, that are gathered or collected from various sources rather than acquired as a whole.

Front cover is an 1889 engraving from the Royal Wedding Special Edition of the Illustrated London News of Airlie Gardens merged with a 2022 photo.

Published in the United Kingdom for:

Friends of Duff House
c/o Duff House
Banff
Banffshire, Scotland
AB45 1SX
FoDH is a registered Scottish Charity reference SC027830

Content copyright ©Friends of Duff House 2022

All rights reserved. No portion of this book may be reproduced, stored in a retrieval system or transmitted at any time or by any means mechanical, electronic, photocopying, recording or otherwise, except for individual personal use, without the prior written permission of the publisher.

First printed 2022

ISBN 978-1-80352-092-6

Researched and compiled by
Ian Williams
Friends of Duff House

CONTENTS

Preface		3
Acknowledgements		5
1.	Introduction	7
2.	John Donaldson	9
3.	Banff in the 1870's	19
4.	Duff House in the 1870's	27
5.	Duff House gardens	35
	A: The Orchard	35
	B: Airlie Gardens	42
	Canal Park	44
	Kitchen Garden	48
	Flower Garden	53
6.	John Donaldson's Diary with notes	63

Indexes

Plants	203
Fruit	209
Vegetables	213
Bible	219
People, places and general	221

1889 engraving of Duff House with lots of guests

PREFACE

In 1984 a surprise package arrived at Duff House, a photocopy of a diary written by an apprentice gardener, John Donaldson. This had been sent from the USA by his grandson, the late Thomas Cureton.

Many thanks are given to Don Aldridge and Charles Burnett, who transcribed the contents in April 2001.

In 2020 the Friends of Duff House made a decision to look at the Diary in further detail. This tied in with the plans of Aberdeenshire Council seeking funding for a refurbishment of the Vinery and Bothy in Airlie Gardens. Funding was sourced for the Vinery and the refurbishment went ahead in 2021 and 2022. This inspiring community space provides opportunities for children, young people and families to take part in valuable health and well-being activities.

The gardens surrounding the Vinery will be brought to life and managed by Greenspace Banffshire.

The original transcript was undertaken before the use of modern computer capabilities were available, and was prepared on a typewriter. This 2021/2 FoDH transcription has benefitted from not only the original transcript but modern technology. This has allowed more words to be recognised – although still not quite 100%!

It had initially been assumed that all references in the Diary to the "Vinery" referred to the very obvious structure in Airlie Gardens. Indeed this Diary is the evidence of when the Airlie Gardens Vinery was built. However, detailed analysis shows that many references to "the Vinery" actually refer to the earlier Duff House garden which also included a Vinery, maintained in parallel to what today is known as Airlie Gardens. The earlier garden was, and is, known as The Orchard – like Airlie Gardens, The Orchard garden has only survived in parts.

John generally distinguishes between the two gardens, often calling Airlie Gardens "the other garden" or "the flower garden" – because The Orchard was much more a producing fruit and vegetable garden. Both had Vineries (ie growing vines), but the Airlie Gardens Vinery is vastly larger, which he often calls the "New" or "Other" Vinery. Both had flower gardens and walks.

I apologise for any mistakes or omissions that may have been made while producing this book and hope you will forgive me. I have tried my best!

ACKNOWLEDGEMENTS

A lot of people have assisted with the research and production of this book for which the compiler is very grateful. The compiler offers sincere apologies to those he may have inadvertently missed out!

Grateful thanks are given to:

National Library of Scotland
Historic Environment Scotland
National Trust for Scotland
Royal Botanic Garden Edinburgh
Scotlands People
National Collection of Aerial Photography
National Galleries of Scotland
Banff Preservation Heritage Society
The Museum of Banff
Macduff Heritage Society
New York City Floral District – James Francois-Pijuan
Tattie Talks – John Marshall
British Potato Trade Association
The Orchard present owners
Innes House
British Police History
chrisgrant.eu (Raeburn)
Clovenfields.net (Vines/grapes)
John O'Neill (Gardenstown)
Biodiversity Heritage Library
Aberdeenshire Council Library Service
The Pelargonium and Geranium Society
National Dahlia Society
James Cocker and Sons

PANSIES.

1. INTRODUCTION

John Donaldson, when he started at Duff House, was 17 years old. He spent just over one year (Oct 1873 to 10th Nov 1874) as a Duff House apprentice gardener, learning his trade. As he states at the start of his Diary, he intends to make this his career. Which he did with spades on (no pun intended)! See Chapter 2 for a summary of his most successful career.

It is clear from the Diary entries that John was serious about making horticulture his career. He clearly was quite studious and learned day by day – not least evidenced by his practice of spelling a plant name as he heard it, but by the next day spelling it correctly – so he either had a mentor and/or access to books and magazines. He visited many other gardens in the area – in fact most times he went to a large estate, he seemed to make a point of visiting it's garden.

His grasp of the English language improves over the year too; it is quite possible that the gardening foreman and/or the Head Gardener, may have helped him. He probably also had access to gardening publications such as the *Journal of Horticulture, Cottage Gardener and Country Gentleman*, a weekly magazine that dealt with all aspects of John's chosen career. Being mentored was not unusual in this profession at the time, and estates such as Duff House regularly took on gardening apprentices. Nationally, gardening apprentices were often encouraged to keep diaries so that they could look back in the future to learn from their previous experiences.

This transcription has corrected some spelling except where John's original adds to the context. John was very poor at punctuation, and his use of capital letters was quite often arbitrary. As seems most logical these have been corrected. He uses local dialect words from time to time and where understood these are explained in the notes accompanying each diary page.

John's day sometimes began as early as 4am. Breakfast was taken after some work, and then followed the period John always calls the forenoon (ie to 12 noon) up to when lunch was taken, which he called dinnertime. The last meal of the day, which John calls tea, was taken about 5pm unless he was invited somewhere to the later meal called supper.

Sundays were mostly, but not always, free. There were occasional other days off, twice a year for a "fast" day, and occasionally because of a celebratory event on the Duff Estate. Apart from these occasional days John took no other holidays – although he does admit from time to time to not really working very hard!

James Duff, 5th Earl Fife

2. JOHN DONALDSON

John was born on 3rd February 1856 - at about 6pm according to the register of births. His family lived at Hillhead of Mountblairy between Banff and Turriff, on the west side of the River Deveron.

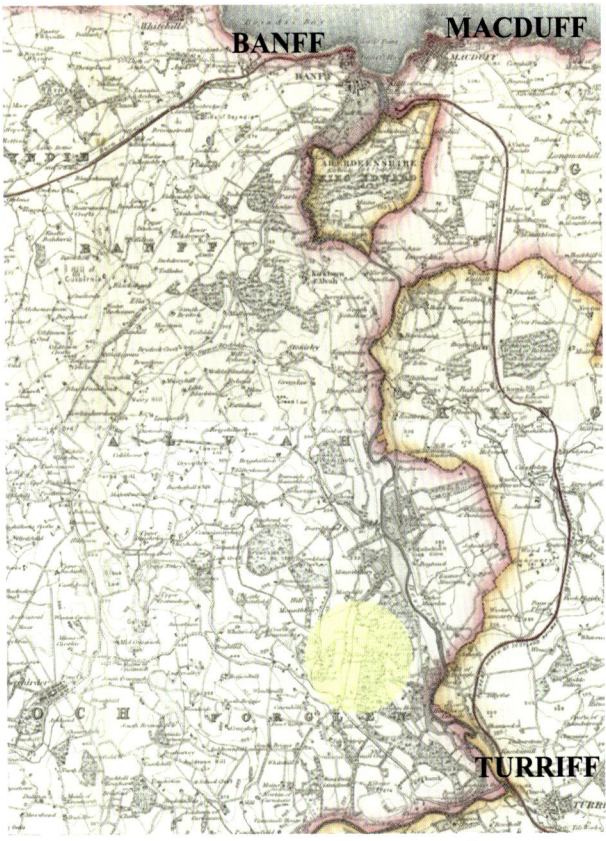

Ordnance Survey 1" map published 1868
Note: the two coloured bounded areas on this map show the convoluted county boundaries at the time; ie King Edward was an island part of Aberdeenshire.
Most of this excerpt is Banffshire.
Reproduced with the permission of the National Library of Scotland

John's parents were George and Jessie (nee McKenzie). George worked on the farm. John had two older sisters, Jessie 12 years his senior, and Christina, 8 years older. His brother James was born four years after him.

Unfortunately by the time John was five in 1861 his father had died, and the head of the household is listed as his mother; his grandmother Janet, and his aunt Christina, were also living with them. His mother was listed in 1861 as a Crofter of 6 acres.

John clearly had some schooling, presumably at Forglen School (now closed). Rev W S Caie was the headmaster, a graduate of Marischal College, Aberdeen.

By the age of 15 John was working as a "Farm Servant" at Westfield Farm in Inverkeithing. Having been brought up in a farming family this was inevitably his first job.

What brought him to Duff House and his decision to make a career in horticulture is not known. But the evidence of his Diary shows how he was very serious about it. Although the Diary starts on 30th October 1873, when John was 17 years old, his career at Duff House probably started up to four weeks earlier, as clearly he was already living in Banff and familiar with his gardening routine. His first Diary entries do not refer to him arriving, or being shown around, so it seems likely he had been in post a little while at least. This is also the conclusion because he was given three months of pay at the beginning of January.

The Diary for his time at Duff House covers just over a year, his last day of work being 9th November 1874, leaving Banff the next day.

From Duff House John went to work at Vogrie House, just south of Edinburgh. Although we have a copy of his diary from his time at Vogrie, it has not been transcribed and is not included in this present publication. His job there seemed similar to that at Duff House, but in an environment where the new house – as below – was being built to replace an older building, and most importantly for John, the landscaped park, it's walled garden and other features, were being developed. The property had been purchased by James Dewar – of whisky fame. Today Vogrie House stands as the centrepiece of Vogrie Country Park, sited between the A7 and the A68 just west of Pathhead.

Vogrie House in 2010 (photo by Ronnie Leask)

After a year or so at Vogrie, John moved on to a large private estate in Yorkshire. He must have then thought his career would benefit from a change or he already had some idea of where he wanted his career to go, so he went to work at Veitch Nurseries in London.

The Veitch Nurseries, started in 1808 in Devon, were the biggest plant growers in Europe around the time John went to work for them. In 1853 Veitch Nurseries expanded eastwards and purchased a large site in Chelsea (no longer there); they were pre-eminent in the horticulture world – presumably something John thought would aid his career.

Veitch in Chelsea was at that time being run by a great grandson of the founder, one Harry James Veitch. They developed many hybrids and employed plant hunters to travel around the world to discover new plants they could bring to the British market – in this they were very successful. There is a six hundred odd page book published in 1906 giving the details of 1,281 plants they introduced!

The Chelsea site closed down in 1914, and the Veitch's original nursery in Devon is now owned outside the family and is known as St Bridget's Nurseries.

Plan of Veitch's original Chelsea Garden

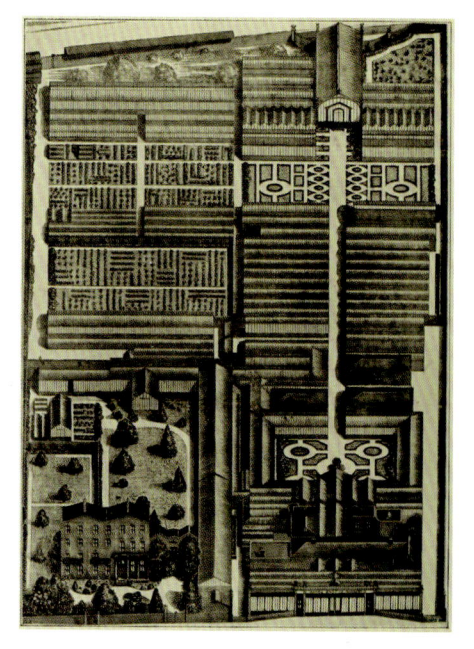

From Veitch's, in 1881 John then moved on to work in the Zoological Gardens in Regent's Park. At that time they occupied about fifteen acres at the north end of the Park – and not to be confused with the Royal Botanic Society who had gardens in the centre of Regent's Park.

The Zoological Gardens were "the pride of London" and were a most fashionable place to visit, especially for the upper classes, "and promenade in its pleasant avenues enlivened by the sights and sounds of a bewildering variety of the animal world."

John presumably was involved in making sure the pleasant avenues remained pleasant!

By 1893 John had set his sights to a different view, and in February he left London for New York. He worked for William Wilson, a well known grower in Astoria, Long Island.

From there he moved on quite quickly to work for T Burroughs Hyatt, who was then starting a commercial cut flower business. John worked for him for six years.

In 1899 John went into business for himself, in Elmhurst Long Island. Although his early career was as an all round horticulturist he elected to be a grower of cut flowers and specialising in carnations and lillies.

One of his several specialities was the Carnation variety "Belle Halliday", at the time revered in the carnation world as the first yellow carnation to have a true deep yellow colour, and for the plant to be able to withstand Scottish, and New York, winters. John didn't develop it, but he became a well-known supplier of it.

Image of "Belle Halliday" from "The Garden" 1885

In London the Covent Garden Market is well known as the major supplier of cut flowers to florists.

The equivalent in New York is the New York Flower Exchange. John Donaldson, all the way from Duff House, was one of the organisers, being it's secretary for 14 years, before becoming it's President in 1912.

The New York Flower Exchange, now the Flower District, started as the Canal Street Floral Market, where traders would congregate to sell their flowers on the day. It was big business; New York at that time was a bit "odiferous" due to poor sanitation and having fresh flowers, cut or potted, helped to mask this.

A busy Canal Street Floral Market in 1871

The Union Square Flower Market developed from this in the years up to 1891. It became very competitive with some sellers even taking others to court over who had dibs on a particular corner spot!

Union Square Flower Market c. 1900

It was into this environment that John Donaldson was starting his own business and, with others, developing the Flower Exchange, so that plants and flowers could be bought in advance and to put some regulation on activities and practices for the benefit of all.

In it's hey day the Flower District spread over several blocks, close to the large department stores of the day; today it is concentrated on West 28th Street.

John Donaldson himself owned a whole block, of 28 lots, in what today is downtown Manhattan. This included three 300ft long greenhouses. As the city developed this land became increasing valuable, and he sold lots off from time to time.

In 1912 it is reckoned that John Donaldson was worth US$ 10 million – not bad from earning £5 a quarter at Duff House!

Apart from his gardening he was a keen and skilled bowler, one of the best in the Astoria Bowling Team. He is mentioned several times in the local papers for his bowling prowess, and described as "a genial and companionable man as well as a good bowler"!

As regards his personal life:

As he wrote in his Diary, John first became a father on 9th Feb 1874. His daughter (Isa)bella was given his family name of Donaldson but was living with her mother, although by 1881 she was living with her maternal grandparents while going to school. By 1891 Isabella was a dressmaker's assistant in Banff. John makes no further reference to his daughter in his Diary after he mentions attending the baptism, but we do know that Isabella married in 1894; she and her husband moved to Dunfermline and had a son and daughter.

In 1887, while he was still in the UK, John married a Banffshire lass. Jane Henry was born in Gamrie, in 1855. By 1871 she was living and working at 4½ Low St Banff in the Chemist shop, owned by Joseph and Ellen Low.

Perhaps this is where John met Jane, but there is no known reference in his Diary; John mentions several young ladies, occasionally with their name but generally just with an initial, so it is difficult to know who they were, or whether a girl mentioned in the Diary became his wife! From transatlantic shipping records we know that as a married couple they returned to the UK a number of times from New York, presumably to see family. So perhaps before he left the UK John was regularly visiting family in Banffshire and carrying on a long distant relationship with Jane. There is no local record of their marriage so we do not know where they were married.

Jane clearly took an active part in the New York Flower Exchange, being on the Entertainments Committee – for events such as their International Flower Show as well as their own Club dinners. John and Jane had two offspring, son Alexander born 1886 (ie while John was still in the UK) who later took over John's flower business in New York; and daughter Ethel born 1896. Ethel's son Thomas was the grandson who sent the copy of the Diary to Duff House in 1984.

By 1920, John (now 64) and Jane moved away from the city but still in New York State; they remained actively involved with the New York Flower Exchange, hosting dinners at their home in Patchogue. They later retired to Florida and by the time he was 85 years old – reportedly in 1940 although that doesn't quite tie in with his Banffshire birth record - John was living with his daughter in Tampa.

John passed away, aged 93, in 1948 (again, the date, not quite tying in with his Scottish birth record).

God Bless John Donaldson, a very successful son of Banff.

John Donaldson in 1912

3. BANFF IN THE 1870's

Banff is factually described as comprising "several well-built streets, with handsome shops, and is remarkably clean and neat" and contains "many fine buildings including the County Buildings". There was a museum, public baths, literary institution, billiard room. custom house, newspaper, county prison, county asylum, life boat, rocket apparatus and coast guard station, and one of the finest hotels in the north. Great North of Scotland Railway trains could be taken either from near Banff harbour, or from Banff Bridge station (on the Macduff side of the river). Buses met every train to all parts of the town and neighbourhood.

All in all, it seems it was a good place to live – and still is !

The sketch below, looking from Macduff, was done a few years later by Elizabeth Robins Pennell, a Canadian traveller.

A bit more detail was given in 1889 when the country's focus was on Banff due to the royal wedding between the sixth Earl and the Princess Royal. A special edition of the London Illustrated News was produced and this contained many sketches of Banff, Macduff and Duff House, including this of Banff from Doune Hill. It is a very fine engraving and almost looks like a photograph!

One of the differences from today's Banff Bridge is that in this illustration the bridge does not appear to have been widened to what it is today; this work was completed in 1881 and hence this drawing must have been done in the 1870's.

The other key difference from today, that is easily visible, is that the main road over the bridge to Banff takes a right turn on the west bank, along what is today Bridge Road, as the only way into the town of Banff. On the Banff side of the bridge there are the pillars, gates and gatehouses of the main entrance to Duff House.

The photo below, from about the turn of the century, is from the Duff House side of the gates, clearly showing the arrangement of the gates. The Duff House drive – the foreground with the two walking ladies - is now the main A98 – New Road – giving an easier route to Banff High Street since 1965. The gates that hung at this entrance – with the gatekeeper holding one open in the photo below – now hang at the entrance to Banff Castle.

A map of Banff Town Centre in 1867 is shown on the next page which highlights the extent – and geographical limitation - of the town itself. The boundary between the town and the Duff estate can still largely be seen today, with the wall opposite the Spotty Bag Shop, and the wall that runs more or less parallel to Bridge Street, between that and the "Temple View" car park. The wall then goes south parallel to Low St, used to go west across what is now St Mary's car park (just to the south of Collie Lodge, which used to be one of the entrance lodges to Duff House), and then can be seen again along the edge of Sandyhill Road (A97 to Aberchirder). This line is shown as a dashed green line on the map – everything to the south of that line was part of the Duff House estate.

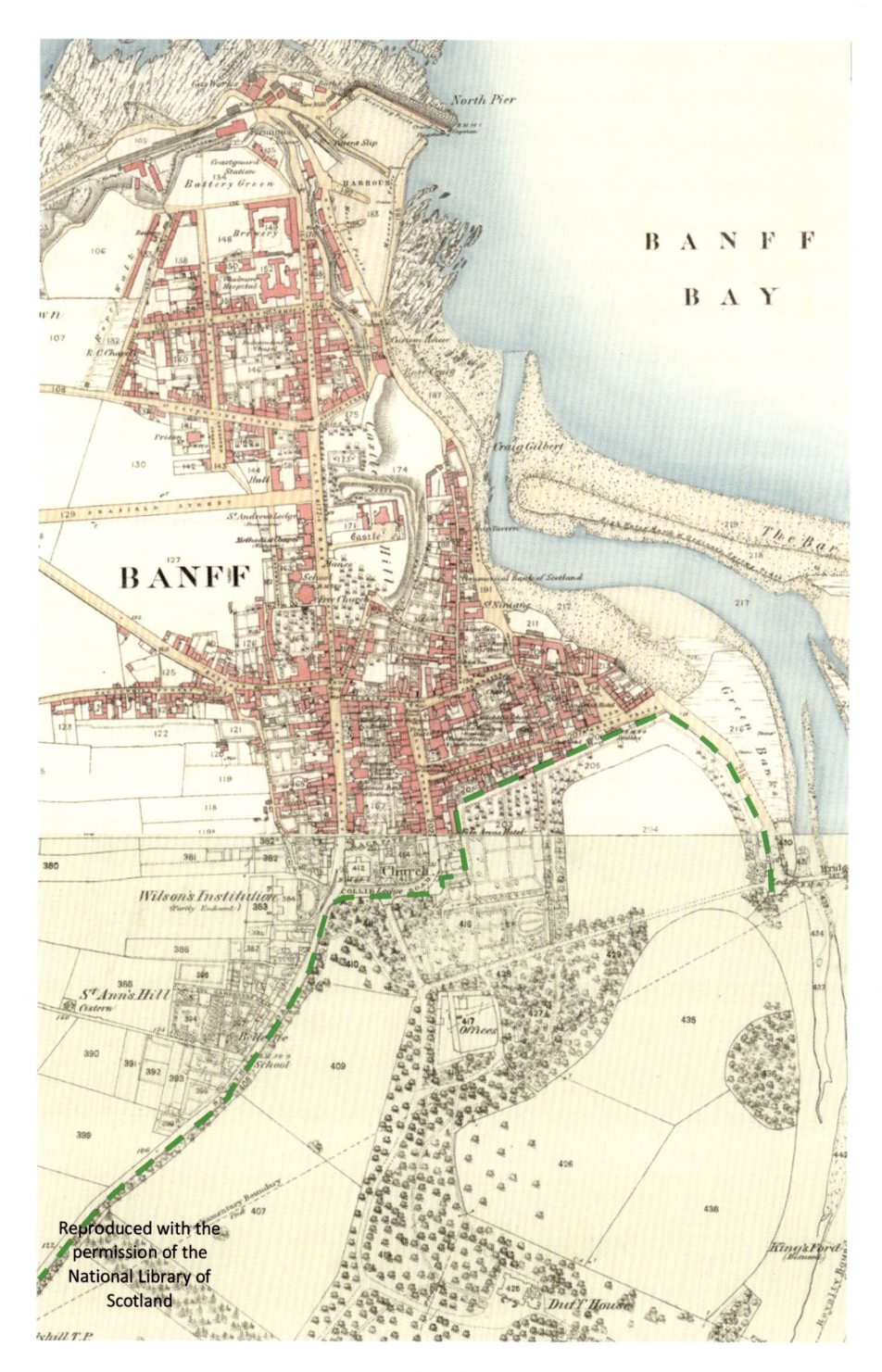

Reproduced with the permission of the National Library of Scotland

This photo shows what is today part of St Mary's car park, with the Duff House estate wall to the right of the photo, and with Collie Lodge to the left of where the horse and cart are. Banff Parish Church is to the left of the picture, with the gate to Duff House in the opening opposite Collie Lodge. The drive towards Duff House is today picked out as the cobbled area across St Mary's car park.

What is today part of Banff Primary School (below, with the Duff House estate wall just visible to the left) is shown on the map as Wilson's Institution, becoming Banff Parish School, headmaster Thomas Gentles.

The map also clearly shows that the River Deveron used to run a different course to the one it has done for the last several decades. The "Bar of Banff", the sand and shingle bar that used to come out from the Macduff side, formed a very useful wind and wave barrier, so that it was effectively a harbour for Banff.

Another key difference from today was the High St; the map shows the road towards the Castle as much narrower than today.

In general Banff High St didn't really look too much different. Of course what is now the Morrisons Daily was not there, but it is still recognisable as Banff High St.

Low Street was not hugely different from today either. Of course the shops themselves have changed, but many of the buildings still exist. The Court House, on the left of the photo below was built circa 1871.

The Directories – and the Valuation Rolls - in the 1860's and 1870's list all the shops and other businesses in the town. The total number of shops in Banff in 1867 (and very similar 10 years later) was exactly 150; that includes all those believed to have a public counter.

In comparison, a fairly recent count of shops, by the same definition, in 2018 was 107; perhaps not as reduced as might have been imagined.

The type of shop has however changed considerably. In 1867 there was just one hairdresser, there were no shops listed as take-aways; there were eight bakers, thirteen clothes shops and even six banks. Today Banff has more hairdressers, more take-aways, but less bakers, drapers and banks, reflecting the change in people's habits over the last 150 years.

The Directories do include "Vintners and Spirit Dealers" but do not have a category for Public Houses. The names of the "pubs" in the 1870's is not really known, although John Donaldson does refer to establishments such as "The Spade", but without saying where it was.

4. DUFF HOUSE IN THE 1870's

The main part of Duff House today is not much changed from how it looked in the 1870's, or indeed many decades before that.

The 1867 map shows the footprint of the House and this clearly includes the east wing, which is sometimes referred to as the "Bryce Wing" after it's architect. This wing had been built in 1870 due to the lack of bedrooms and facilities in Duff House itself, this arising because the original William Adam designed east and west wings had never been built due to a dispute over the cost of building the main house.

Apart from what has until recently been the café in Duff House, with it's adjacent kitchen, the original design for the House had all kitchen and related facilities in the west wing. Because this was never built, a series of separate structures just to the east of the House had been used over the years. Initially these had been at least six feet (two metres) from the main house, due to the risk of fire; but the Bryce Wing was properly attached as not only maps show, but as the architects drawings show (on the next page).

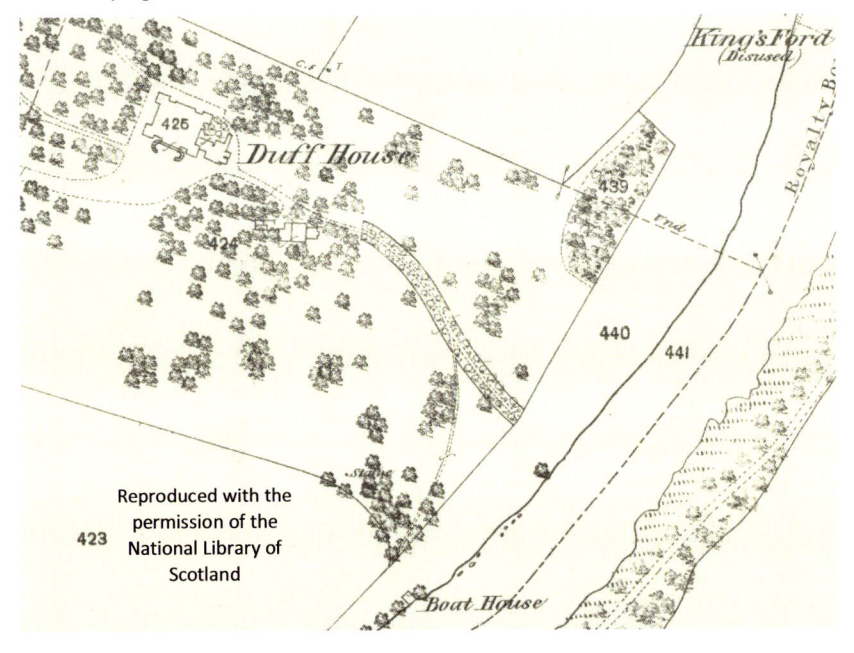

Reproduced with the permission of the National Library of Scotland

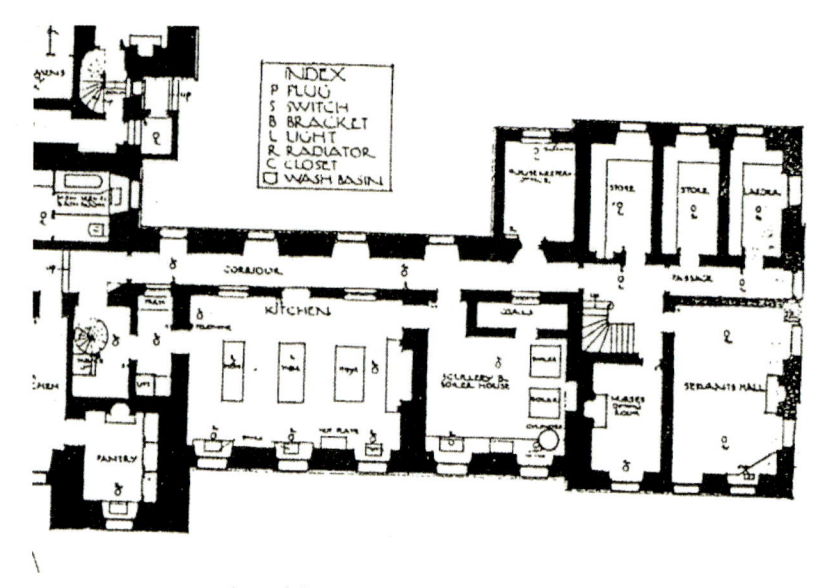

Plan of the 1870 "Bryce Wing" ground floor.
Note that the 1867 map gives a different outline because at that time the construction of the wing was started, but not completed. Photos from the 1950's confirm the above plan is correct.

This "Bryce Wing" was bombed on 22nd July 1940 and demolished in the 1950's. During the construction of the joint British and German War Memorial in 2018, placed exactly on the southeast corner of the "Bryce Wing" close to where one of the bombs fell, the foundations were found where they had been expected.

This is a drawing done of Duff House, from the town side, in 1871 which appeared in the Illustrated London News. Although it gives something of the correct situation, it is somewhat inaccurate in detail, including how many windows Duff House has horizontally (should be nine, only seven drawn!).

One of the other features on the map is the Boathouse. Duff House and the Bryce Wing can be seen in the background in this photo.

Another feature shown on the map is a "Statue", seen in this 1779 sketch extract, but clearly still in place at the time of John Donaldson.

The 1867 map also shows some buildings to the southeast of Duff House, in amongst the trees. There is no record as to what these were used for and no sign appears to exist today; perhaps they were for some of the staff, noting that there were few rooms available in the main house. This is also the area in which it is believed the Nissen huts used during World War Two were placed (for which some of the concrete foundations used to be visible a few decades ago).

The line of trees, with a track through the middle, leading to the southeast of the House down to the River Deveron, is believed to be the track to the "Fishers Gate" that John Donaldson refers to in his Diary.

The "King's Ford" across the river used to be the main ford across the River Deveron for the towns people, before Banff Bridge was built and before the Duffs owned all the river frontage. The first map showing any ford is Roy's map of Scotland of 1747, but this is clearly a ford across Scury Island. The King's Ford links to a track on the Macduff side, some of which can still be traced. The first Banff Bridge was opened in June 1765, but was washed away on 17th September 1768. The present Banff Bridge was in use from 1779.

The alternatives for crossing the river without a bridge were either a ferry, but "not a single year passed without some unfortunate occurrence at this ferry". Or the ford further upstream across Scury Island, linking the Duff House estate to the tracks around Kirkside Farm. The Bridge of Alvah – within the Duff House estate – was only built in 1772, between the two Banff bridges.

Living at Duff House in 1873 was the current Earl Fife, the fifth Earl, James Duff. He was the nephew of the 4th Earl Fife, Alexander Duff. The family tree of the Earl Fifes is shown below:

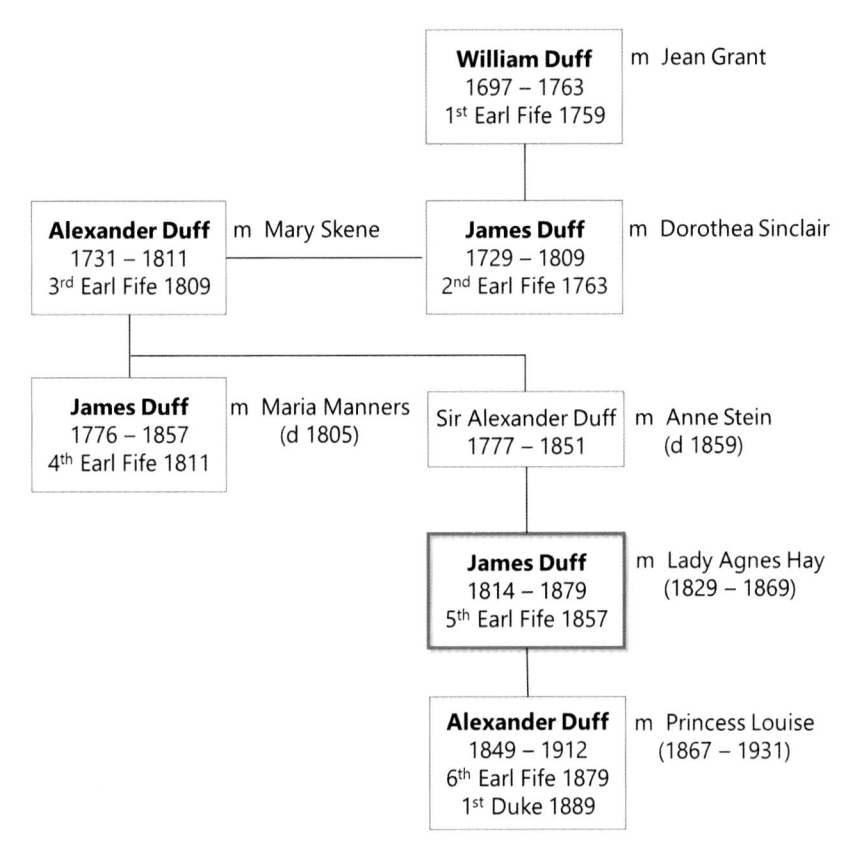

```
                    ┌─────────────────────┐
                    │   William Duff      │  m  Jean Grant
                    │    1697 – 1763      │
                    │ 1st Earl Fife 1759  │
                    └──────────┬──────────┘
                               │
   ┌──────────────────┐        │        ┌─────────────────────┐
   │  Alexander Duff  │ m Mary │ Skene  │    James Duff       │ m Dorothea Sinclair
   │   1731 – 1811    │────────┴────────│    1729 – 1809      │
   │3rd Earl Fife 1809│                 │ 2nd Earl Fife 1763  │
   └────────┬─────────┘                 └─────────────────────┘
            │
   ┌────────┴──────────┬───────────────────────┐
   │   James Duff      │ m Maria Manners       │ Sir Alexander Duff │ m Anne Stein
   │   1776 – 1857     │    (d 1805)           │    1777 – 1851     │   (d 1859)
   │ 4th Earl Fife 1811│                       │                    │
   └───────────────────┘                       └──────────┬─────────┘
                                                          │
                                               ┌──────────┴──────────┐
                                               │    James Duff       │ m Lady Agnes Hay
                                               │    1814 – 1879      │   (1829 – 1869)
                                               │ 5th Earl Fife 1857  │
                                               └──────────┬──────────┘
                                                          │
                                               ┌──────────┴──────────┐
                                               │  Alexander Duff     │ m Princess Louise
                                               │   1849 – 1912       │   (1867 – 1931)
                                               │ 6th Earl Fife 1879  │
                                               │  1st Duke 1889      │
                                               └─────────────────────┘
```

Duff House was not Lord Fife's only home. The Banffshire Journal does make mention from time to time that Lord Fife was in Banff, and from the Diary we know he spent time at Innes House near Elgin. When he was younger he spent time living at 30 Pall Mall in London, and also at Delgatie Castle between Banff and Turriff.

He had married Lady Agnes Hay in Paris in 1846 but unfortunately she had died in 1869. They did have five surviving children including the one son, Alexander, who succeeded his father in the Earldom.

By the time of John Donaldson's Diary in 1873, all of the children were fairly grown up:

1. Lady Anne Elizabeth Clementine Duff, born 1847, had married in 1865;
2. Lady Ida Louise Alice Duff, born 1848, also married;
3. Alexander William George Duff, born 1849 – the future sixth Earl Fife and first Duke of Fife, referred in John Donaldson's Diary as Lord Macduff, the traditional title of the eldest son being Viscount Macduff;
4. Lady Alexina Duff, born 1851, also married;
5. Lady Agnes Cecil Emmeline Duff, born 1852. There is no mention of her at Duff House in John's Diary, and it seems she lived mostly in London.

There are a few images of Lord Fife, James Fifth Earl. This marble bust is in Duff House, believed to have been sculpted in 1861 by Alexander Brodie.

James was also the Lord Lieutenant for Banffshire, and Knight of the Order of the Thistle (as shown by the star he is wearing in this picture).

The Order of the Thistle is a Scottish order of chivalry, consisting of the Sovereign and sixteen Knights and Ladies - plus some royal family extras.

The picture to the right is of Viscount Macduff – the future sixth Earl Fife and future 1st Duke of Fife - around the time of John Donaldson's Diary.

Lord Macduff did visit Duff House from time to time, and the Diary covers both his 24th and 25th birthdays (10th November). In 1873 Lord Macduff's birthday gave rise to a special celebration with the gardeners, although a large formal party was held on the occasion of his 25th.

The oldest son of the current Earl is traditionally given the title of Viscount Macduff, and that entitles him to be called Lord. Alexander William George Duff born 10th Nov 1849 was the holder of that title for the duration of the Diary, becoming Earl Fife on 7th Aug 1879 in the Irish peerage, then Earl of Fife in 1885 in the peerage of the UK, and on 29th July 1889, two days after his marriage to Princess Louise he was elevated to the Marquess of Macduff and the Duke of Fife, and in 1900 the Earl of Macduff to ensure his titles could pass to his daughters, as he had no sons. Today, the previous titles have lapsed and the current Duke of Fife is also the Earl of Macduff.

Before the time of the Diary, Lord Macduff must have lived for a while at Innes House. Amongst the many treasures there is a bit of an insight into his childhood, written from Llanbryde Parish School on his 9th birthday. They thank Lord and Lady Fife for their interest in the school and hope that Viscount Macduff has many future happy birthdays.

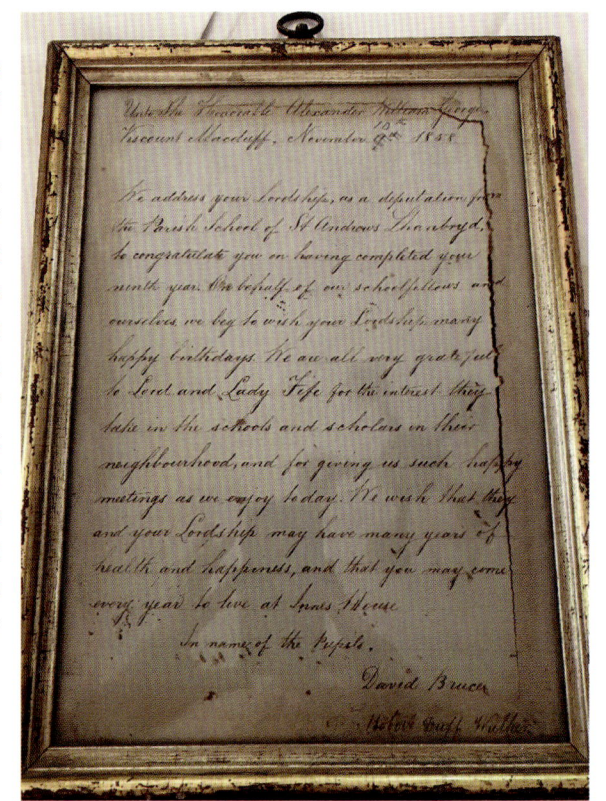

5. DUFF HOUSE GARDENS

There were two garden areas that Duff House maintained during the nineteenth century, The Orchard and 10 acres near the town, of which Airlie Gardens today was part of.

A. THE ORCHARD

The Orchard first appears on a map as some form of cultivated area in 1747 – around the time that Duff House building was being resumed after the battle of Culloden. The map is General Roy's map, itself prepared as a direct result of Culloden and the Jacobite uprising, so that future troop movements in Scotland would have some guidance as to the best routes.

On this map – 1747 - an orchard is depicted as ordered trees, with two fields to the east, with a cluster of cottages to the north and south of it, all entitled Sandyhills. "Braco's House" is shown, ie Duff House.

There is a map of Banff of 1775 and although some of Lord Fife's lands are shown, the whole area is just shown as "Grounds adjoining to Duff House", as the map was made for Lord Findlater!

The next map of any useful scale is one drawn by Duncan in 1858 – Duff House Grounds - with an extract below courtesy of Banff Preservation and Heritage Society. The Mausoleum (built 1792) is near the bottom left corner of this extract, and the Ice House to the right, just above the centre line. These two known features identify the location and confirm it is the Orchard, consisting of an ordered set of trees, with a cultivated area to the west of them.

The first Ordnance Survey map, from a survey of 1861 confirms this although the scale is considerably smaller.

The next survey is 1867, again by the Ordnance Survey and at a very good 25 inches to a mile (but scaled for the extract below).

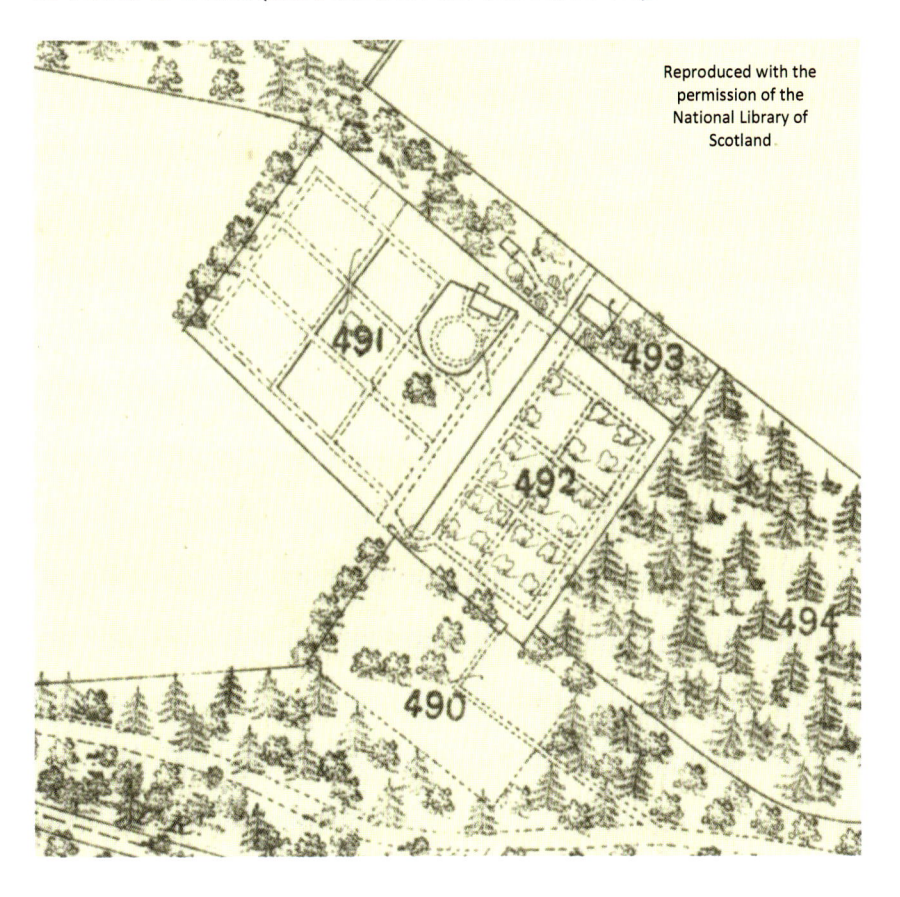

Reproduced with the permission of the National Library of Scotland

The orchard part (labelled 492) is reduced in size from the previous maps but corresponds exactly with what is on the ground today.

However, much of the vegetable garden (labelled 491) is now part of the field to the west and some of the buildings are much changed. The drawing on the next page is an overlay of a more modern map (in red) on the 1867 one as above.

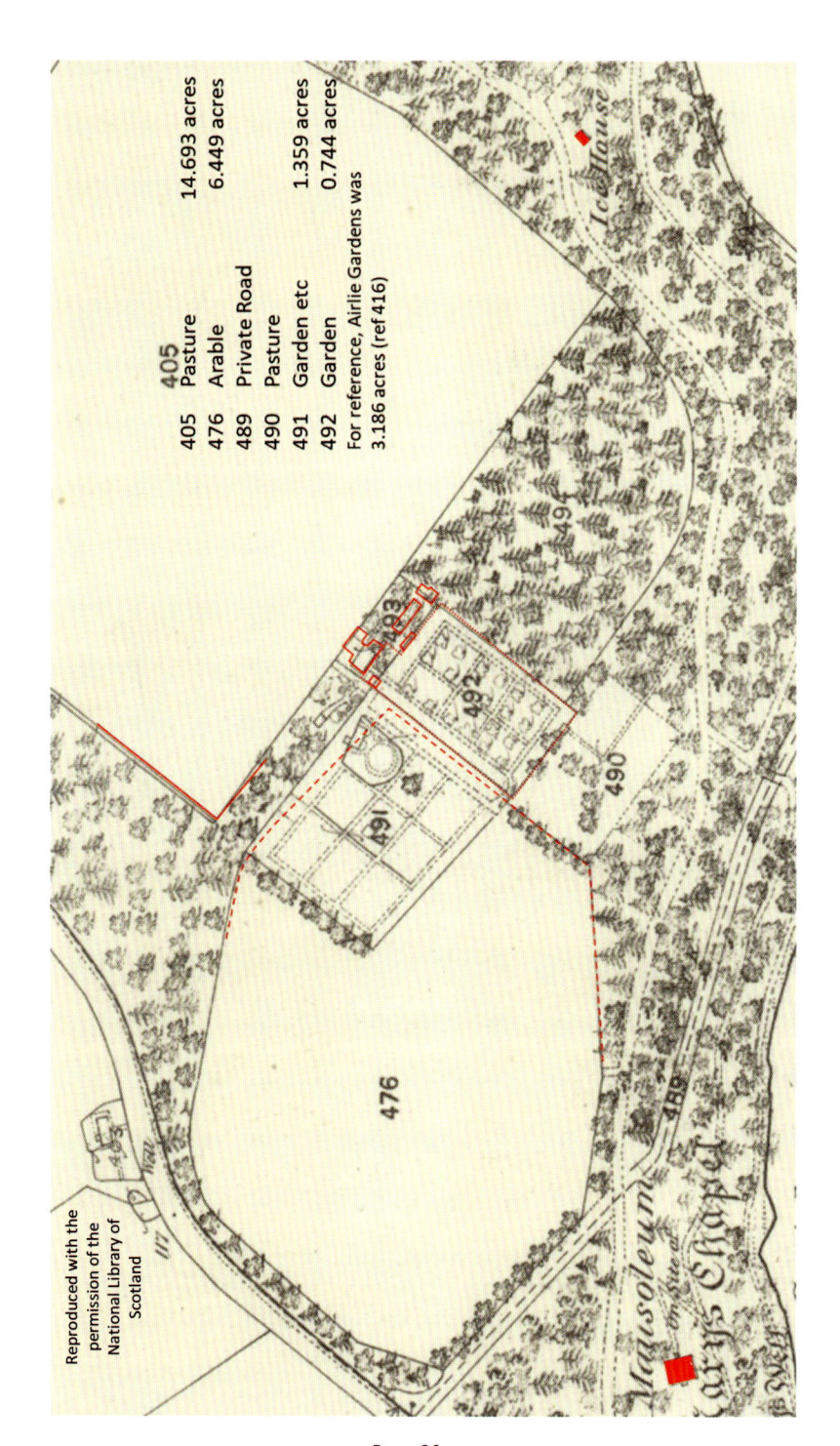

405
405 Pasture 14.693 acres
476 Arable 6.449 acres
489 Private Road
490 Pasture
491 Garden etc 1.359 acres
492 Garden 0.744 acres

For reference, Airlie Gardens was 3.186 acres (ref 416)

Reproduced with the permission of the National Library of Scotland

However, surprisingly 150 years on since John Donaldson lived and worked at the Orchard, there is much still in existence:

- the wall between the orchard and vegetable area still largely stands;

- the site of the Vinery, with some of it's back wall, is still visible, and really surprising two vines are still growing, even without the protection of a greenhouse today. Refer to the note opposite the page for 26th Oct of the Diary in Chapter 6, to read about the possible identification of these vines.

- When at Airlie Gardens, John lived in the Bothy built on the back of the Vinery. This is a substantial building with several rooms and clearly suitable for accommodation. At The Orchard there is a Bothy behind the Vinery, but this is tiny and it seems unlikely to be human accommodation. It seems more likely that John and others were housed in the building surrounded by a wall within the vegetable garden, now demolished.
This Orchard Bothy now has a cement washed original wall, but retains what appears to be the original slates and a Victorian era roof light.

- the "Cow Shed" as it is called now is also original with a more modern roof and windows, with various original internal fittings.

- A few of what appear to be old fruit trees are also still growing, and fruiting (to some extent). The layout of the rest of the orchard area can still be seen.

The site now has a substantial house, the largest of the buildings (in red) on the overlay map. This was not there when John Donaldson was, but it does incorporate a barn structure that was.

There is no sign of the path that is shown on the map going southwest from the bottom corner of the orchard, although the gate posts in the wall are still there.

The vegetable garden area was very productive based on John Donaldson's entries. Refer to Indexes for a full list of vegetables, fruit and flowers that were grown at Duff House.

B. AIRLIE GARDENS

What is today known as Airlie Gardens is really only one part of what used to be a much larger Duff House gardens. The first map that was drawn including any level of detail was one made by John Wood of Edinburgh, A Plan of the Town of Banff dated 1823.

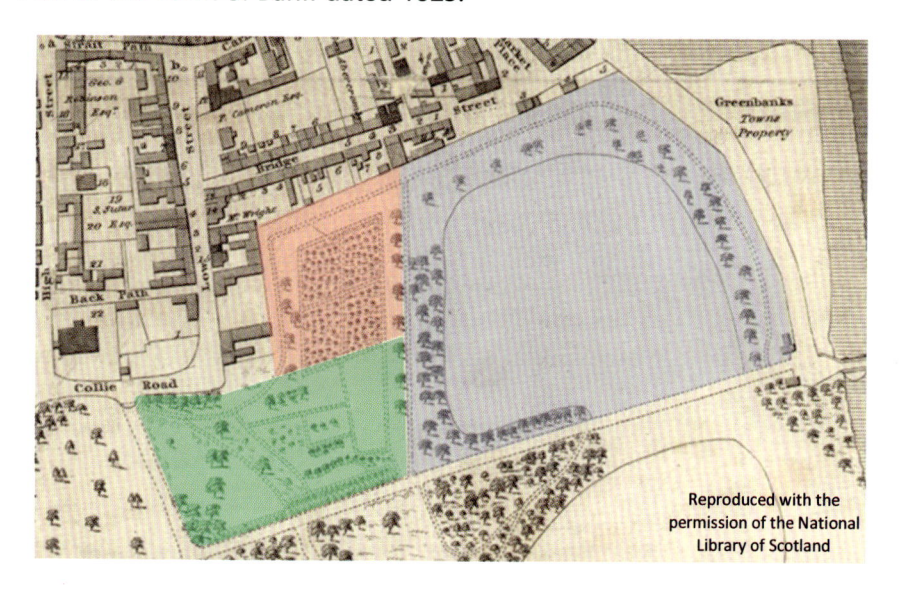

Reproduced with the permission of the National Library of Scotland

There are some reasons why there is some doubt around the detailed accuracy of this Plan (see below), but it is the right proportions and fits what can be seen elsewhere as a generic layout.

The overall gardens are perhaps best considered in the three areas it was naturally split into in the mid 1800's, highlighted above:
- 1/ Canal Park - towards the river (blue);
- 2/ Kitchen Gardens - east of Low Street (red);
- 3/ Flower Garden - Airlie Gardens or today (green).

The next page is a comparison of 1867 and today, followed by sub-sections considering the history of each of these three areas in turn.

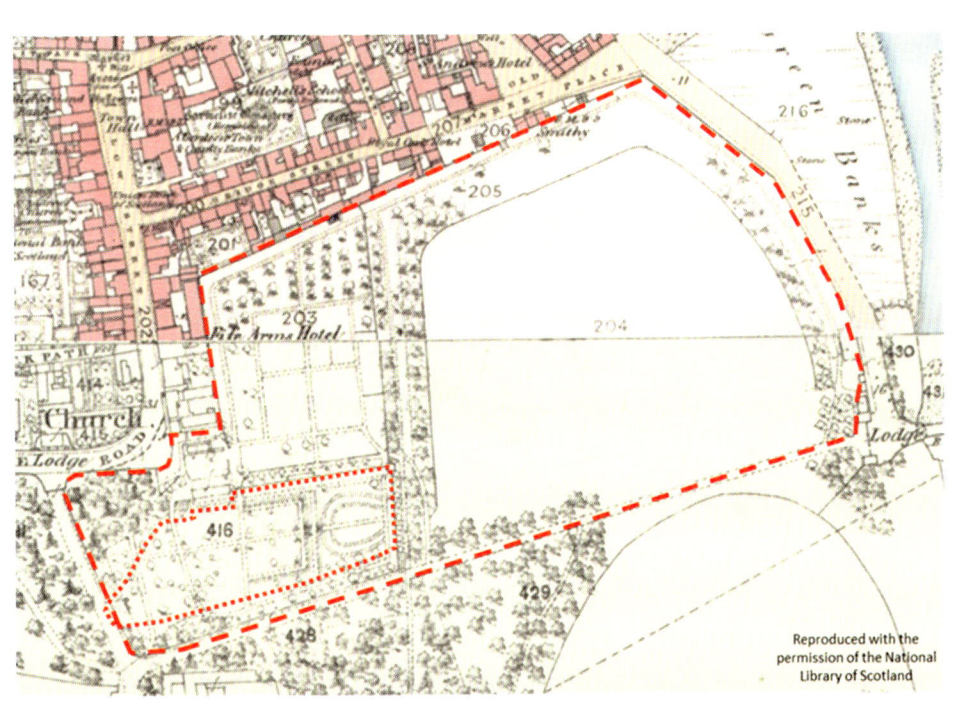

Reproduced with the
permission of the National
Library of Scotland

Imagery ©2022 CNES/Airbus, Getmapping plc, Maxar Technologies, Map data ©2022

5 B.1 Canal Park

One particular feature in 1873 that John must have kept a weather eye on at all times was the Head Gardener's house. John often refers to Mr Mackie, and his wife and family. They lived in a house that adjoined the small pavilion that is still in place, that had been on one side of the Duff House gates by the bridge – in what today is part of the Co-op car park. It is shown on the 1873 map, and from an account almost one hundred years earlier it was built sometime in the early 1700s. Seen on the left of this turn of the century postcard. It was taken down in the 1930's.

The field, now called Canal Park and Princess Royal Park, is to the left of this photo. This is the area that has the present day football pitches, as well as where the tennis courts are. It had a path around it, and shrubs to the side. *Refer also to a Ch 6 note for 6th Dec 1873.*

From photos and postcards – such as the one on the next page - it seems that the main part of the field was used for sheep at times.

And as shown on the photo and the 1902 Ordnance Survey map (below), some areas started to be fenced off.

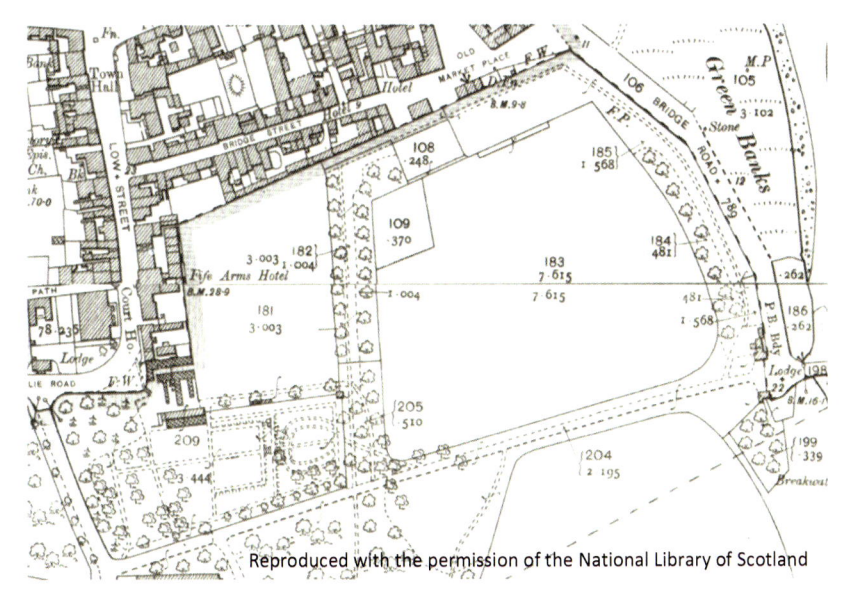

Reproduced with the permission of the National Library of Scotland

In 1906/7 the Duke and Duchess of Fife gifted Duff House and much of their estate, including the Duff House gardens area, to the Burgh Councils of Banff and Macduff, for use as golf and other recreational purposes. This commitment was underlined by the Provosts of the day, and to a large extent the purpose expressed by his Grace, the Duke of Fife, has been followed.

This field was then used for one football pitch, initially placed at an angle;

And then straightened up, much as now, with the new Drill Hall also having been opened in 1925, and the tennis courts.

By the 1950's there were two pitches;

In 1965 New Road – now the A98 – was completed,

The trees between this field and the more formal gardens to the west were removed, leading today to the Princess Royal sports ground and the Canal Park area, both being very popular football areas.

5 B.2 Kitchen Garden

The 1823 map suggests that the gardens had not been particularly developed, but had been laid out.

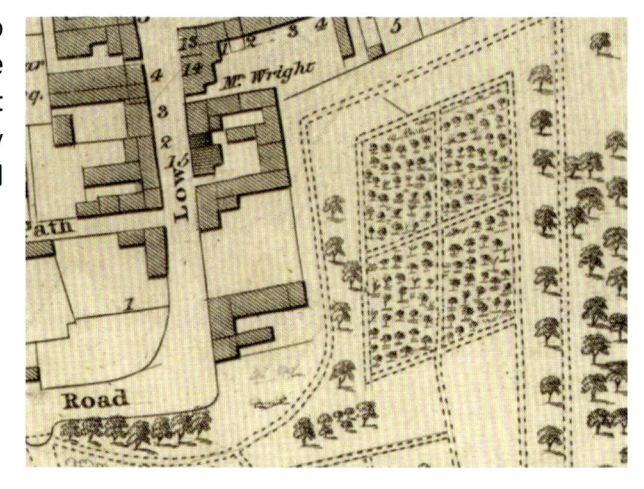

Both maps reproduced with the permission of the National Library of Scotland

But by 1867, with the Fife Arms now built on Low Street, this area of garden had been developed and more formally laid out.

John Donaldson refers to the back of the hotel a number of times in the Diary. He calls this area the Kitchen Garden.

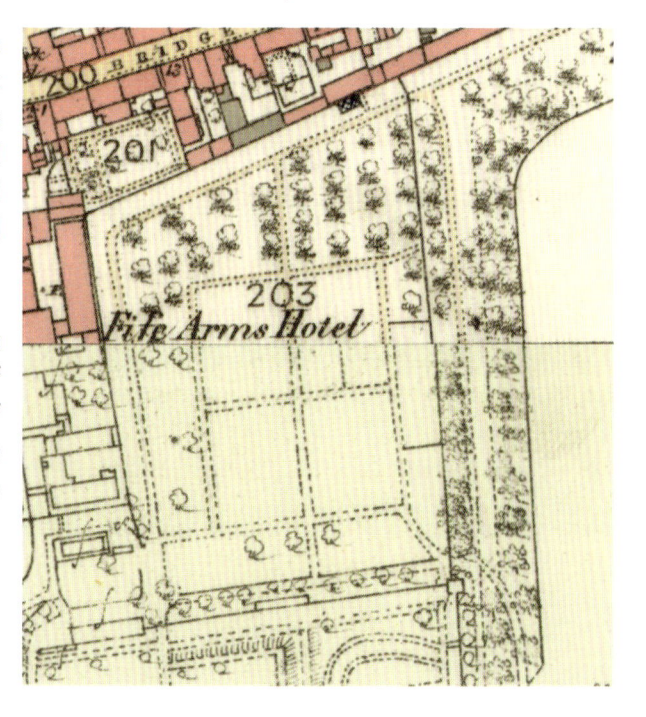

A photo taken likely towards the end of the nineteenth century shows – looking through the trees – that the layout was as the map shows, a square pattern of paths/beds.

However, by 1902, the next detailed Ordnance Survey, the area – 3 acres - appears to have been cleared.

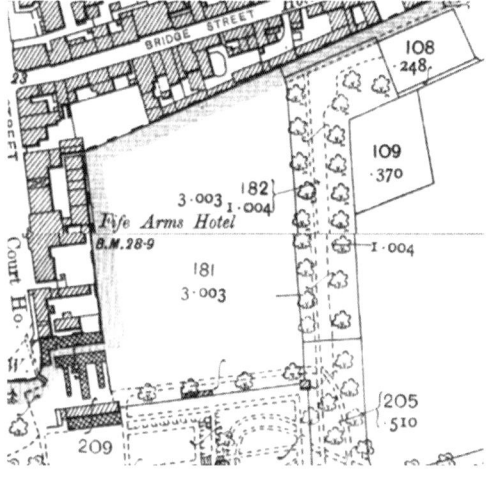

Reproduced with the permission of the National Library of Scotland

Notwithstanding the 1902 Ordnance Survey map, aerial photos taken in 1928 and 30th April 1948 clearly show some planting in place.

Photos reproduced under licence from Historic Environment Scotland.

The Fife Arms Hotel acquired this garden at some point, both for a source of fresh fruit and vegetables for use in the hotel, but also for guests to walk around. The year is uncertain, but it is a similar layout to the aerial view above in 1948.

Into the 1950's and the trees between the football pitch and the gardens have now been removed.

This area is now Airlie Gardens and Temple View sheltered housing, built in 1985.

A modern view of the Flower Garden looking towards what used to be the Kitchen Garden, now Sheltered Housing.

5 B.3   Flower Garden

So called because originally Airlie House was built on the upper part. There is one painting that shows Airlie House and it's surroundings:

Reproduced by kind permission of The Museum of Banff

William Duff's father, Alexander purchased this in 1692 from the Ogilvy family – the Earls of Airlie and the Lords Banff. This title lapsed in 1704 after the last of the family died.

Initially it seemed that William Duff (later 1st Earl Fife) might refurbish Airlie House, but obviously finally elected to build Duff House from scratch.

Airlie House, or the "Lodging of Airlie" was sited on the upper part of what is today Airlie Gardens. The upper flight of steps in the middle of today's Airlie Gardens is made of stone and these were the original entrance steps to Airlie House.

Other surviving parts of Airlie House are believed to be the six statues that now adorn the front and back of Duff House – or rather the original lead versions of these; the ones now on Duff House are glass fibre replicas. Two of the originals are in Duff House and the other four have been refurbished and are in Historic Environment Scotland storage. An account in 1743 records these as being taken from the Bowling Green at Airlie House, now the lower part of the modern gardens.

The six of these statues still surviving are as follows.

Facing the front of Duff House, left to right:

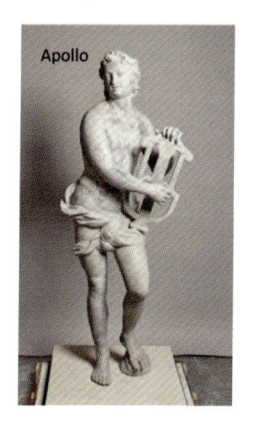

Mars

Apollo

Minerva

Facing the back of Duff House, left to right:

Bacchus

Mercury

Diana/Luna

Page 54

These statues also come with a mystery. In other places around Europe this sort of collection of statues of the gods sometimes come as a dozen, rather than just six. Certainly 12 would seem a more likely number to adorn a green the size of the lower part of Airlie Gardens.

The 1743 records refer to taking the statues and placing them "on the House and the temple". The only known "temple" would be the "Temple of Venus", and thus might indicate there were originally more than six statues, as in past times the Temple did have a statue inside!

Airlie House was still standing in 1746; it was being used by the grandfather of James Imlach (author of a history of Banff in 1868) who "for some years" had been superintending the building of Duff House. This year was of course that of the battle at Culloden, effectively ending the Jacobite rebellion. The Duke of Cumberland was the commander of the Royal army and marched into Banff on 10th November 1746. William Duff allowed the Duke and his senior officers to use Airlie House as their temporary headquarters, and the army to camp in his new Park surrounding Duff House. Duff House at that time was unfurnished and not finished.

It is believed sometime after 1759 before 1779 Airlie House was demolished. Although Duff House was built by then, the stables, later offices as well, at what is today Duff House Royal Golf Club seemed to have re-used some of the Airlie House stonework. In 1916 while fitting out some of the buildings as a Nurses Home, fifteen fragments of carved stones were found. One had the whole word "LODGING", others with letters of NG, I, O or G, I and D; also one with "61" on it, perhaps a date of 1561 or 1661. These letters do not all fit "Ogilvy" or "Ogilvie" but could also be part of their predecessors the Bairds.

The next visible record of Airlie Gardens is circa 1805 in a painting by William Hay of the "The Town of Banff". The image below is from a hand-coloured engraving of that by John Clerk.

Reproduced under licence from Historic Environment Scotland

This shows the tower, still existing in the northeast corner, and the wall heading towards St Mary's, at this time with two sheds leaning up against it. The tower has not had a roof for many decades, but note that in the painting, showing Airlie House (above), the tower is roofed. It is also roofed in a Cordiner watercolour of 1780.

Interestingly another tower is shown in this 1805 painting. By zooming in it can be seen this appears to be a doocot, with one sloping roof towards the north. A similar "lectern" style doocot can be seen just off the A98 nearing the Portgordon junction, built by the Duke of Gordon family on their Leitcheston estate. Doocots were a means of farming doves for food.

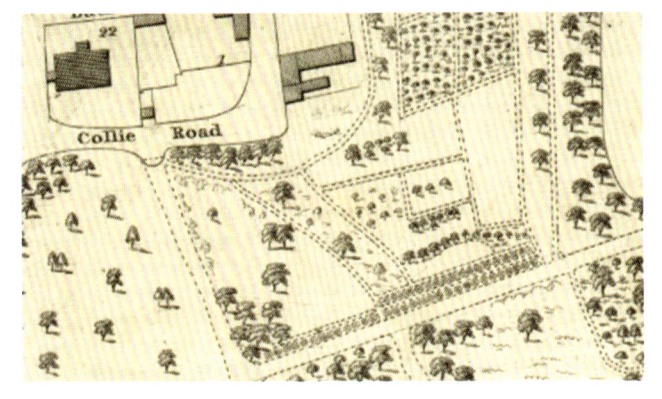

This 1823 map by John Wood does not show the tower, nor the wall leading from it to behind the present Vinery. It seems more likely these are inaccuracies rather than actuality, since the wall is clearly there previously. The 1805 painting doesn't show east, west and south walls and it is thought these were only built circa 1860 in preparation for the planned gardens.

The driving force behind the remodelling of the Flower and Kitchen Gardens in the 1860s it seems was Lady Agnes, wife of the 5th Earl. She also had plans for immediately in front of Duff House, but after her death in 1869 those plans were dropped.

By the 1867 the walls are clearly shown by the Ordnance Survey. The map below gives a detailed layout of the now developed gardens, with a surrounding wall on all four sides of the Flower Garden. The doocot presumably went during the garden layout works.

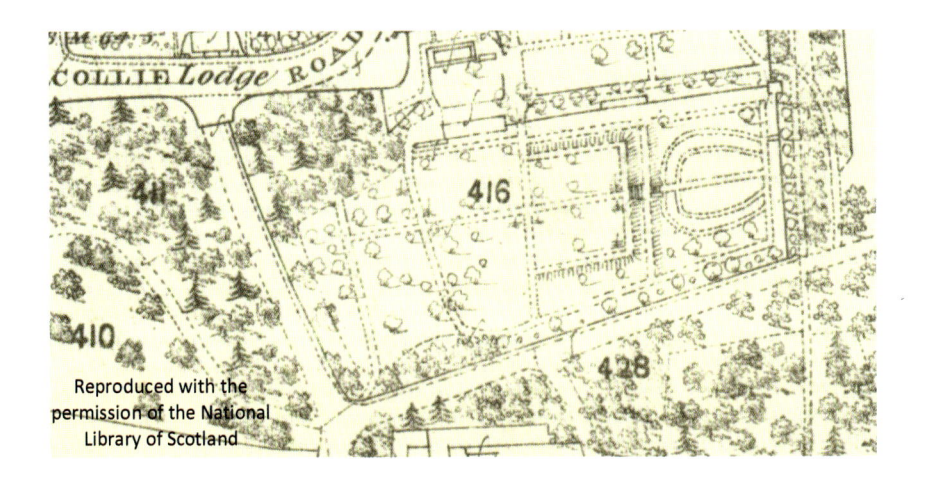

Reproduced with the permission of the National Library of Scotland

Based on John Donaldson's mentions in his Diary, the layout of Airlie Gardens is very similar to that shown on the 1867 map, although there are two differences:
- the Vinery is not yet built (1872), although there is a building of some sort;
- there is a structure immediately to the north of this, which was called the "Palm House".

Next to nothing is known about the Palm House, but it couldn't have been very large. From the double lines on the map it was not large; in comparison to the Royal Botanics Gardens Palm House in Edinburgh (built 1834) is was about one fifth the size.

John makes no mention of this so perhaps it had been removed when, or before, the new and present Vinery was built in 1872. It had initially been thought this might have been 1873, however as grapes from the New Vinery won at the Banff Show in 1874, and the first year's grapes should not be picked, it must have been built in 1872! This is backed up by Mahood in his 1919 book "Banff and District".

By 1902 the Ordnance Survey map shows the Vinery, and the same layout of Airlie Gardens as 35 years previously, although the buildings directly to the north, where the Palm House was, are completely changed. They are depicted as glass houses – quite an extensive array. This was just four years before Lord Fife announced he was handing the estate to the Burghs of Banff and Macduff.

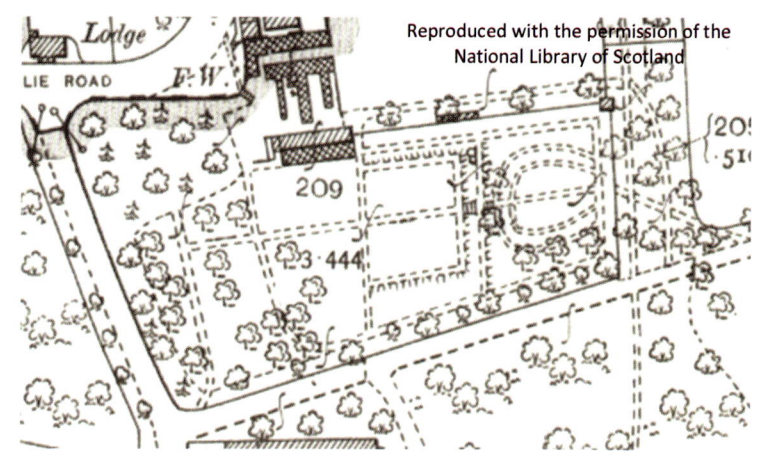

Reproduced with the permission of the National Library of Scotland

Page 58

The known layout of the Flower Garden in the time of John Donaldson at Duff House is as per the sketch below.

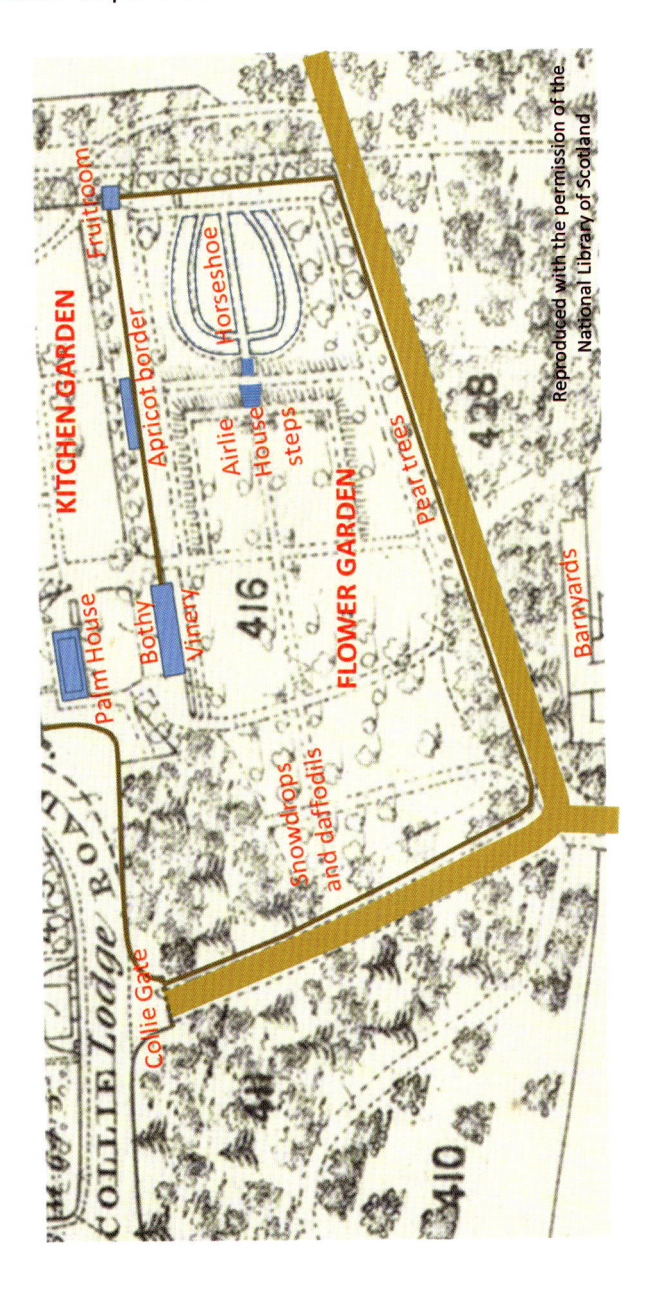

A photo likely to have been taken right towards the end of the nineteenth century however shows Airlie Gardens themselves not looking particularly cared for, but does give a hint of glass houses through the trees below the church.

The next detailed map is 1929. The ownership has now passed to the Burgh Councils. The map still shows the glass houses to the north of the Vinery, but also an additional one to the south, in the middle of what is today the top part of Airlie Gardens.

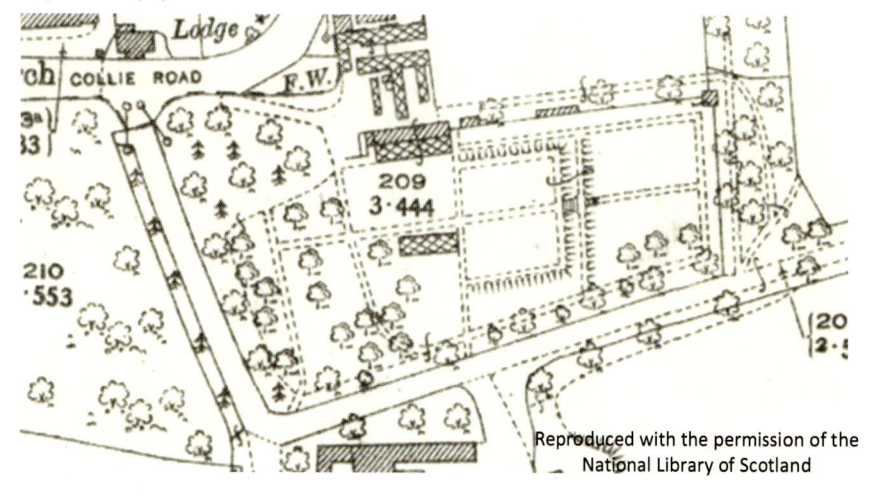

Reproduced with the permission of the National Library of Scotland

With all the glass houses already there it would seem an obvious choice for the area to become a Market Garden, at some time before the photo below taken 1928.

This shows both Airlie Gardens with it's additional greenhouse, the existing greenhouses, and the layout of the two garden areas.

By the late 1960's it seems as though this had all fallen into disrepair.

The gardens reverted to public gardens, seemingly in stages:

6 John Donaldson's Diary with notes

The Diary was written in a plain note book in which he drew a left hand margin on each page, not a pre-printed diary as can be purchased today. He always filled every page, putting the month and dates at the top of the page, and then using the margin to note the day of the week. From time to time he includes other marginal notes, sort of headlining his entries, presumably with the aim he could more quickly find things in the future. He starts the Diary by saying it is for his own use and not for anyone else so the layout only needs to suit him. Sometimes he includes just three days on a page, sometimes seven or more, obviously depending on how much he wrote. In this transcription, for layout reasons, we have not followed the same number of days per page as John did, but otherwise the transcript is complete.

His punctuation is often non-existent and so in this transcription the best meaning has been used. His use of Capital letters on words is also very variable, always used at the start of a sentence, but because he uses them for many words they are no indication of a new sentence!

His spelling improves throughout his year at Duff House. A number of interesting spellings are highlighted by our Notes, but perhaps a good indication of his dedication is that he rarely gets it wrong a second time. He comes across as diligent and either looks up the plant name - and certainly there were libraries throughout Banff to which he would have had access, and probably within the Duff House estate too. Also, it is likely he received mentoring from either the Head Gardener, Mr Mackie, or perhaps from his foreman.

Almost every day ends with a summary of the weather; "rough" meaning windy, and "fine" meaning low wind.

The Notes we have included are on the right hand page with relevant words or phrases highlighted in blue on both the left hand page transcription, and in the Notes on the right hand leaf. Occasionally notes are not alongside their dates due to space, but reference is given.

Occasionally there is word that we have been unable to identify or find the background to; these are highlighted in pink.

John Donaldson's Diary starts as follows:

It appears to be a very difficult task for me to get a commencement on this book but as I don't intend to write this for public inspection it does not matter what I commence it with. And as I don't intend to commence an old month on this half sheet I will put down anything that turns up in my memory while I am here.

30th October

1873 Thu: We dug the raspberries yesterday the 30th October 1873. I was over at Macduff last night at a lecture delivered by Mr Bruce from Banff, subject "The Wise Men of the Nineteenth Century." It was very good and very short for we was little more than half an hour kept.
The chairman intimated to us that another lecture would be the week after - I forget who was to deliver it - but the subject is the Newspaper Press.

31st October

1873 Fri: We put the potatoes into the pit, 40 different varieties, and a good many not put into the pit. Some like rain in the morning but cleared off throughout the day but we had a good shower at night.

Mr Bruce, the Rev William Straton Bruce, was the Minister of Banff Church. He was a long time Minister in Banff, arriving here in December 1871 and ordained 6th March 1873. So when John Donaldson went to his lecture Rev Bruce had only been here seven months or so. He had been educated and trained in Aberdeen and Edinburgh and was a very learned gentleman, publishing many papers and books; however his biography "Bruce of Banff" makes it clear that he was exceptionally diligent in his work as a Minister. He visited every household in Banff parish once a year, every communicant twice a year, and several times a week visited the sick. He was minister until 1925 but continued to live in Banff until 1931, moving in with his widowed daughter in Edinburgh, and died in 1933. He had married a Banff girl, and they had five sons and four daughters.

Rev Bruce did write diaries for much of his life but unfortunately most of them were destroyed, although various quotes are included in the 1934 Rev Ferguson's Book "Bruce of Banff".

This painting was by John Bulloch Souter made in 1924 and is currently in the care of Aberdeenshire Council. *See also 14th June.*

A potato pit or clamp is one method of storing potatoes once harvested. Typically this is done by laying the potatoes on straw, covering the tatties with more straw and then several inches of earth. This keeps the potatoes dry, cool (but not frozen) and out of the light. This method can store tatties for several months. The Diary entry for Nov 3rd 1874 includes a nice expression, to make sure a rotten potato doesn't ruin the store: separate "the godly from the unjust" before the potatoes are put into the pit!

Two specific varieties are mentioned on 15th Oct 1874 - see note for them.

Potatoes were a major crop at Duff House and they are tended dozens of times throughout the Diary.

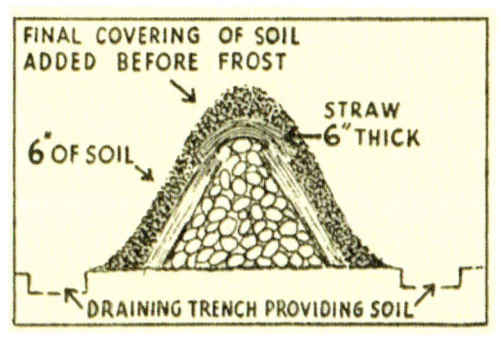

Extract from WW2 "Dig for Victory"

1st November
1873 Sat: In the morning we tied up some currants and gathered some flowers for the House. After breakfast we cleaned the Walk of the Flower Garden of leaves. Then took vegetables to the House. His Lordship came today so we have been very busy. A very rough raining day.

2nd November
1873 Sun: Was down with vegetables in the morning. At Church in the forenoon. Text: Col. chapter 3 and versus 2,3 and 4.

3rd November
1873 Mon: Down with the vegetables in the morning. At the Ice House twice after breakfast. Cleaning the Walk between the Fruitroom and the Bothy. In the afternoon Mr R and Mr B was down covering Mr Mackie's potato pit. There was 2 degree of frost this morning but been a fine day.

4th November
1873 Tue: Down at the House with vegetables in the morning. Cleaning Mr Cleland's dunghill forenoon and digging the Apricot border. After dinner at the Ice House. Two degrees of frost this morning but has been a fine day. The first day of the shooting.

5th November
1873 Wed: In the morning down at the House with vegetables. After breakfast up at the Ice House and at the Orchard for more onions and saw Mr Mackie cutting the last of the grapes. Took up the dahlia roots and gladiolas today. My first lesson on singing from Mr Pirie last night and was practising the bass of the tune Badeus. Two degrees of frost this morning but been a fine day till the evening, there was a good shower.

His Lordship would be James, the 5th Earl Fife (as in this portrait by James Faed, courtesy of NGS), widower of Lady Agnes (died 1869). *See Chapter 4 for more information.*

One of the duties of the Gardeners was to keep the House, ie Duff House, supplied with the vegetables and other garden produce that they needed, and so John was often down with vegetables.

Collossians Chapter 3, vs 2-4 reads "Set your affection on things above, not on things on the earth. For ye are dead, and your life is hid with Christ in God. When Christ, who is our life, shall appear, then shall ye also appear with him in glory." King James version, as in use in the Church of Scotland in 1873.

The Ice House is quite a well known feature in Wrack Woods, just off the track to the Duff House Mausoleum, with access to go through what used to be a double air lock and look into it. This one is built of brick into the side of the hill, with a drain for the melting ice at the bottom. It is unusual in that it is egg shaped. *See the note against 19th Feb 1874.*

The Fruitroom was the castellated building still in Airlie Gardens. *See Chapter 5 for a garden layout.*

The Bothy is the building behind the Vinery, built especially for the gardeners to live in. They were therefore on site to keep the fire for heating the Vinery going, and it provided a warm back wall to the Vinery. This has of course been magnificently refurbished during 2021/22 and is now in community use.

A potato pit has a note for 31st Oct 1873 (and again mentioned on 15th Oct 1874).

Badeus   One aspect of a hand-written diary is that some words are going to be hard to decipher, especially when they relate to things that have perhaps gone out of fashion. When transcribing this Diary an alphabet of ways John wrote his letters in known words was created, and using those examples this word seems to be "Badeus", but this is not a familiar song now and a search did not find anything relevant. Just the fact that John was taking part in town life shows how rounded he was trying to make his life.

6th November

1873 Thu: In the morning was down with the vegetables. After breakfast, up at the Ice House. Tied the dahlia *talia's* in the Vinery, made room for the cutting boxes. Cleaned the potato shed. A bad day most extraordinary.

7th November

1873 Fri: Got no rest last night for the rain pouring down on me and the wind till my shirt was sticking to my back with wet. In the morning down with vegetables as usual. After took the cutting boxes to the Vinery, cleaned them of leaves. After dinner at Ice House. Last night I was in with Mr Hardy visiting Mrs Cleland and the family. Got an introduction to Miss Smith. Music on the piano, some singing and other amusements from 7pm till 11. After we went home with Miss S. returned and I went to bed. Been a very rough rainy day today.

8th November

1873 Sat: Down with vegetables in the morning. At the Ice House after breakfast. Took up some savoys from the Canal Door to the herb border. Took the frame and sashes to the potato shed and the frames down to their winter's residence. Sent a hamper of onions down to the House to go with the carts to Innes House on Monday morning. Been a very rough cold day.

9th November

1873 Sun: Down at the House the forenoon. At Church in the evening. Text 14th chapter St John, Verse 6. A fine day.

For Nov 5th 1873 John refers to dahlia roots, but the next day he seems to use the word "Talia". The suspicion is that this is the first example of John hearing a word, but not knowing how to spell it. Hence John perhaps meant "Tuber" but spelt it "Tuba". In other examples he later uses the word again and spells it correctly, although not in this instance. There was no known variety of dahlia called "Talia" at the time (although one was created in the 1990's in the USA).

Mr Hardy appears to have been John's foreman, but who leaves in a few days time (10th Nov 1873). Mr Hardy's boss was Mr Mackie, the Head Gardener.

Miss Smith only appears this once in the Diary. John was it seems quite a one for the ladies, and quite a few get mentioned throughout the Diary, frequently only once. Two other mentions of the name "Smith" do occur; a fellow gardener and a strawberry grower.

The night of 6th when John got soaked in the Airlie Garden Bothy and most of the day on 7th Nov 1873 were indeed rough rainy days. Reportedly the Deveron was at the highest level for several years, and illustrated by the bridge over the river at Turriff which was completely submerged converting "it into one sheet of water".

The Canal Door was so named because of the Canal that used to run from downstream of where Banff Bridge now is, to the back of Duff House. This was built during the construction of Duff House, so that ships (often the Earl Fife's own) carrying stone from William Adam's facility on the Forth, could tranship onto barges for easy transport to the building site. This was of course filled in, but on really wet days the approximate line of the canal can be seen across Royal Duff Golf Course. This is the derivation of the name of what is today known as Canal Park. *See Chapter 5 for a garden layout.*

Innes House is another of Lord Fife's houses, in this case towards Elgin. The family spend Christmas 1873 at Innes House. *See note after 31st Dec.*

14th chapter St John, Verse 6 reads "Jesus saith unto him, I am the way, the truth, and the life; no man cometh unto the Father, but by me." The "him" is Thomas – often known as "Doubting Thomas" as he doubted the resurrection of Jesus without seeing his wounds. The question that Jesus was answering from Thomas was "We know not whither thou goest; how can we know the way?".

10th November
1873 Mon: Over at the station with Robert Eana. Cleaned the cabbage border, cut the asparagus, cleaned out a cauliflower frame, dug and planted it and planted the remainder at the bottom of the Apricot Wall, also some phloxes planted at the wall, had over four plants to the supper table which was tonight in honour of Lord McDuff's birthday. Fine day.

11th November
1873 Tue: Over at the Banff Station to see Mr Hardie off. Took up some plants to send away to Mr Mackie [at] Buckie and to Mr Shand some Chrysanthemums. Took some Sir Astner, Dactillis and Penstemons and planted them in at the dyke side by the tank. Sent away the hampers that came with the vines to Dr Thorpe. No singing tonight. Fine day.

12th November
1873 Wed: Put in some more Penstemons, Blue Salvia up at the wall side and cleared out the Horseshoe. Took down what was in it and here they are Cerastium at the outside, Verbenas next, but they did not do well at all. Blue Salvia next did very well. Trentham Rose Geranium did well. Antirrhinum they did not do well; a lot of them did not come and we had no others to fill up the space. African Marigolds do very well for the centres, scarlet Penstemons next, Jonquilla, Calceolarias, Dwarf Nasturtium, Alyssums. The insides of the Shoe looked very well. A fine day.

13th November
1873 Thu: In the morning went round the gardens with the new foreman. After breakfast clearing out the beds in the Flower Garden. At that all day. A fine day. Flitted up to the Orchard.

Robert Eana. The surname is not all clear, but appears to be a four letter word beginning with E. He may have been another apprentice, as in a year's time a number of staff are leaving, and this Robert may be one of the previous years' apprentices.

Apricot Wall *See Chapter 5 for a garden layout.*

Lord McDuff (correctly spelt Macduff, and as John uses in later examples) is the title given to the eldest son of the current Earl Fife. In 1873 he was 24 years old. The supper was a special occasion in the grounds for the employees with Mr Mackie in the chair. *See also Chapter 4, and the note for 6th Dec 1874 when his 25th birthday was celebrated.*

Sir Astner is a great example of John's developing garden knowledge. Note that the next day he then spells the name of the plant correctly, Cerastium also known as "Snow in Summer". The first time it seems John wrote it down as he thought he heard one of his colleagues, or perhaps his Foreman, say it; but by the next day John had spoken to someone or looked it up.

The Horseshoe was a major feature in what is now the lower Airlie Gardens. *See Chapter 5 for a garden layout..*

Trentham Rose Geranium. By the nineteenth century there were at least 500 varieties of geranium known in the UK. Trentham was a well known Hall and garden, near Stoke on Trent, the home of the Dukes of Sutherland. At the time of John's diary the head gardener there was George Fleming. A very influential person in the world of gardening, and his team there developed a number of geraniums.

Although the "Register of Pelargonium Cultivars" maintained by PAGS (Pelargonium and Geranium Society) does not include the "Trentham Rose" it is referred to in the accounts of Trentham Hall. George Fleming used to send his planting plans each autumn to the Duchess of Sutherland and on one occasion he refers to "Trentham Rose" and "Trentham Scarlet"; that year he used 100,000 plants of 110 varieties!

George Fleming's bed layouts were much admired; he developed the style of ribbon planting, lines of the same plant. Trentham gardeners had to "dress the beds" every fortnight to make sure the ribbons remained separate. The 1873/4 Horseshoe planting plans (*see 12th Nov and 21st May*) were ribbon designs. *See 16th March for another named Geranium used in the 1874 plan..*

Flit: to leave place, to go elsewhere; to move house.

14th November
1873 Fri: First day at the Orchard. In the morning went to St Mary's Well and some little jobs. After breakfast raking leaves all day. In the South Border of the Flower Garden. A fine day but no sun for three or four days back.

15th November
1873 Sat: Down at the Williams'; had got the gun mended. I went out to Lyons for powder. Was raking leaves all day. Shot a hare at dinnertime, a fine day. Mr Mackie away at Ardmiddle today.

16th November
1873 Sun: Went down to Gardenston with Mr Wiseman. Was at the new church in the forenoon. Minister preaching the text from 7th Chapter Deuteronomy the 20th verse. Saw Miss D at the chapel at six o'clock. Was home about 9pm.

17th November
1873 Mon: Changed the hours today. Down about 9. Raking leaves up in the wood today and down at the end of the Flower Garden. Commenced on the grass. Been a fine day for the leaves.

18th November
1873 Tue: Raking leaves all day. Was out at dinnertime and saw Miss D. Received a present from her. Has been a fine day.

The Orchard is not a well known place today, but was in fact the first garden for Duff House. Some of the garden layout still exists today, but the buildings have changed considerably. The property is privately owned and the author would like to thank them for their kindness in showing him around and for allowing photographs to be used. *See Chapter 5A.*

St Mary's Well still exists. It is a hillside spring around which a stone structure has been built, said to contain the font from the old St Mary's chapel (where the Mausoleum is). The stonework is currently poor and access extremely difficult. It is sited approximately 75metres south of the Mausoleum, below the present "footpath" that goes down to Hospital Island.

Lyons was a hardware and sporting shop at 28 Low St (the junction of Bridge St and Low St). It continued to exist until the 1980's. The present building was only put up in 1900. This photo shows the original single storey shop.

Ardmiddle used to be a large house estate, with a walled garden, greenhouses and much else, situated just west of Turriff. The house and virtually all of the immediate gardens were demolished in the 1950s and there is hardly any visible sign today. It used to be the home of a Mrs Milne, but a school for up to 100 children from 1874.

Gardensto(w)n New Church is believed to mean the "new" Mohr Church, built 1830s over a mile inland, now a private dwelling, as opposed to the old Mohr head church, St John's, now ruinous. *See note after 31st Dec.*

7th Chapter Deuteronomy the 20th verse "Moreover the Lord thy God will send the hornet among them, until they that are left, and hide themselves from thee, be destroyed". "them" being the land of Egypt with "evil diseases".

Miss D appears four times in John's diary. She appears to be named later on as Miss Davidson (*3rd Aug 1874*).

Changed the hours refers to a change of working hours due to the onset of winter darkness. Daylight saving (summer) time in the UK started in 1916.

19th November
1873 Wed: Throwing up leaves at the dykeside and digging flower beds in the Flower Garden. A fine day.

20th November
1873 Thu: Took down the potatoes in the morning and then went to the digging in the Flower Garden and was at that the rest of the day. Been a fine day.

21st November
1873 Fri: Digging in the Flower Garden in the forenoon. At the market in the afternoon. Not a very big market and not a very fine day.

22nd November
1873 Sat: The forepart digging the Borders at the end of the Flower Garden. Burned some rubbish up in the wood. In the afternoon we covered the pit at the Fruithouse. Lord Fife came today.

23rd November
1873 Sun: Been a very rough day and raining sometimes. Was at Macduff Church in the evening. Text was from 1st Chapter of Corinthians, the 23rd and 24th verses.

24th November
1873 Mon: Went up to Raeburns in the morning for gloves and was pruning the rest of the day. Cold towards evening. Pruning today all day. Our new apprentice came today. A fine day.

25th November
1873 Tue: Took down a barrowful of onions to the other garden, spliced the cutting of verbenas and some other little affairs. The rest of the day pruning. Fine warm day. Gather some button onions at the Orchard when we came home.

A dyke is wall made of stone or turf. The Flower Garden is believed to be a reference to Airlie Gardens, ie the area that used to be completely walled on four sides, and with the Vinery.

There was a weekly market in Banff for corn and provisions held on a Friday. This photo is the "Old Market Place" around the turn of the century.

The Fruithouse in the main Duff House gardens was the castellated corner tower that is still there.

Lord Fife, the fifth Earl Fife, James. *See Chapter 4 for more information.* The Banffshire Journal reports:
"The Earl of Fife, Mr and Lady Alexina Coventry, Lord Kilmarnock, Hon. Hamilton Duncan and Mrs Duncan, Mr Arthur Coventry arrived on Saturday at Duff House from Innes. Mr Tayler of Glenbarry and Col Duff of Knockleith arrived yesterday on a visit to the Earl of Fife; and Mr Douglas Ainslie of Delgaty and Mr Grant of Glengrant are expected today."
Some of these guests, together with Lord Macduff with Sir George and Lady McPherson Grant of Ballindalloch were last week on a visit to Rothiemay House (the home of Mr and Mrs Tayler of Glenbarry). "The party had excellent cover shooting."

The Minister at Macduff Church was Rev William Hunter. This church was much the same as today, the spire and extensions having been removed in 1865.

1st Chapter of Corinthians, v 23 and 24. Seems most likely to have been Corinthians 1: "But we preach Christ crucified, unto the Jews a stumbling block, and unto the Greeks foolishness; But unto them which are called, both Jews and Greeks, Christ the power of God, and the wisdom of God."

William Raeburn was a Nursery and Seedsman (and Wine Merchant!) at 28 High St, Banff. No 28 is today what was the Episcopalian Church Rectory, but in the late nineteenth century house numbers on High Street (and Low Street) were changed. What was 28, became 81. *See next page for more background on Raeburns..*

26th November
1873 Wed: Pruning blackcurrants all day but an hour after dinner that we gathered the withered leaves off the plants in the Vinery. A fine day, but a few showers and a cold evening.

27th November
1873 Thu: Pruning blackcurrants all day. Fine day but some showers.

28th November
1873 Fri: Pruning blackcurrants in the forenoon. Raking prunings after dinner and wheeling on the stuff out of the drain till dark. Some showers today.

29th November
1873 Sat: Spreading the stuff out of the drain among the berry bushes, taking out the old willow root out of the corner. Commenced to dig among bushes after dinner. I was over with some snowdrops and planted round Wm Craig's grave, after picking withered leaves off the plants in the Rowans. A rainy afternoon.

30th November
1873 Sun: At Church in forenoon. The Minister from Fordyce, the text was in John 4, 10th verse. Was over at Macduff in the evening and the text there was Colossians Chapter 1 Verse 5. A fine day.

1st December
1873 Mon: Digging all day among the gooseberries. A fine warm day, the thermometer was at temperate today.

81 High Street – the old 28 - is the corner of High St and Boyndie Street.

In fact, in 1873 when John Donaldson went to Raeburns for his gardening gloves, the shop, although listed in various directors as "William Raeburn", it was his son Charles who was running it, his father having died in 1868.

Charles had been working for one of the leading Seedsmen in the UK, Peter Lawson and Sons, but returned home as his father was ailing, and Charles and his wife Margaret took over the shop. With his experience from Lawsons Charles made an excellent Seedsman, and with his wife running more of a grocery shop alongside, the business did very well, and Charles became very well respected.

A shop under the name of Raeburn continued to at least the 1950's in Banff.

> **NOTICE.**
>
> CHAS. RAEBURN, in tendering his thanks to the friends and patrons for the liberal patronage bestowed on his late Father during the past thirty-one years, begs respectfully to intimate that he will carry on the business as formerly, under the Firm of WILLIAM RAEBURN & SON, SEEDSMEN AND FLORISTS, GROCERS, WINE, AND SPIRIT MERCHANTS, and hopes, by strict attention to business, and the supplying of Goods of the best quality, to be favoured with a continuance of that support accorded to his late father.
>
> W. R. & SON beg to announce that they have received a choice selection of TEAS, &c., which they can with confidence recommend, and solicit attention to the following prices:—
>
> **TEAS.** Good Strong Congou, 2s. 6d. to 2s. 9d. per lb.; Superfine Black Tea, 3s. per lb.; Finest Kaisou, Souchong, and Moning Tea, 3s. 4d. per lb.
>
> **COFFEE.** Finest Mocha and Jamaica, 1s. 6d. and 1s. 8d. per lb.; Choice Mixed, 1s. 4d. and 1s. 6d. per lb.; Smith's Essence, 10d. and 1s. 8d. per bottle.
>
> **SUGARS.** Crushed, 4½d. and 5d. per lb.; Fine Loaf, 5½d. and 6d. per lb.
>
> Also, SOAPS, SPICES, PICKLES, FRUIT, CORN FLOUR, RICE, MARMALADE, and all other requisites in the Grocery Trade, at equally moderate prices.
>
> WINES, SPIRITS, &c.; Old Crusted PORT and Golden SHERRY; Renault's, Hennessy, and Martell's BRANDIES, GINGER WINE, CORDIALS, of Sorts, and ORANGE BITTERS; Bass & Co. and Allsopp's ALES, Edinburgh ALE; Barclay & Perkins' London and Guinness' Dublin PORTER.
>
> 28 and 29, High Street,
> Banff, September 1868.

William Craig is mentioned just this once, but John visits William's mother three times later on (7th Dec, 14th June and 29th Jun). William obviously meant something to John, but we can't track down anyone of that name who died after John was of any age. Snowdrops grow abundantly in Wrack Woods, so digging a few bulbs was an easy task for John. *See note for 29th June.*

The word Rowans is not very clear but it certainly is not Vinery. We don't know if this was the name of some sort of greenhouse, or an area of the Orchard garden.

The Minister from Fordyce was the Rev James Grant. John Ch 4 v10: "Jesus answered and said unto her, If thou knewest the gift of God, and who it is that saith to thee, Give me to drink; thou wouldest have asked of him, and he would have given thee living water."

Collossians Ch 1 v5: "For the hope which is laid up for you in heaven, whereof ye heard before in the word of the truth of the gospel;" Colossae was part of the city of Rome.

2nd December
1873 Tue: Digging all day. I received a letter from Australia today. A fine day.

3rd December
1873 Wed: Digging among the blackcurrants today. Planted the Gushet Corner where the willows was with blackcurrants. Got a newspaper from Australia being a day after the letter. Mackie brought up some grapes that came from Tweed Vineyards and a pineapple - the first of them that I ever saw. Price £1 and 8 shillings. A nice day.

4th December
1873 Thu: Digging the redcurrants and young gooseberries. At the back of the hotel killed a pig. To Mackie's tonight. Going with a flower to some young ladies that is going to a ball as I got a small note out of a window yesterday with some conversation lozenges but did not notice the note that was in it till tonight. I noticed it in the envelope. A splendid day.

5th December
1873 Fri: Digging the rhubarb today. A fine day.

Getting a letter from Australia was presumably unusual for John; we haven't been able to find any relations that emigrated, but doing so was quite common in the second half of the nineteenth century. Perhaps it is this sort of background that later didn't make going to the USA a major issue in John's mind. 1873 Australian stamps still bore the head of Victoria.

A gushet corner is a triangular corner. The maps don't show any triangular corner, but the reference to willows suggests it was in the south corner of the Orchard garden, as there is a drain (a ditch). From later entries, currants are grown in both the upper and lower Orchard gardens.

The Tweed Vineyards were THE place for the growing of vines. William Thomson started his vine growing business in 1868 in Clovenfolds in the Tweed valley just west of Galashiels. For 80 years it was very successful. They are not in existence any more but there are a number of available records, and their telling of how to look after vines seems to have been a similar method to that used at Duff House. Presumably bringing grapes to show John, was Mr Mackie's way of showing him what his vines were meant to be producing! *See note on the page for 26th Oct 1874..*

Pineapples have been known in the UK since 1668, originally known as the King Pine. Not many are likely to have been known in Banff.

The Duff House gardens ran along the back of the Fife Arms Hotel on Low St. How a pig came to be there is not certain as it was generally a cultivated area! *See note against 5th Feb 1874 for further info..*

Conversation Lozenges were a forerunner to the "Love Hearts" sweets of more recent times. A confectioner in York, Joseph Dobson, started producing them as a clever marketing product. Joseph was well connected in the industry, having married the sister of one of the founders of Terry's of York, one of the well known sweet manufacturers.

John doesn't say what was in the note, but it was a splendid day!

6th December
1873 Sat: Cutting some weeds on the border that goes round to Mackies. Took them off and wheeled on the stuff that came out of the drain on both sides of the Canal Door and took some hurliefuls of gravelly stuff from the top of the drain and put it on the walk beneath the Canal. A fine day frosty towards evening.

7th December
1873 Sun: Over at William Craig's mother's after dinner. Was at Church in the evening. Mr Bruce preached from the 1st chapter of John, 10th verse.

8th December
1873 Mon: Taking up leeks all day. We had Mr Milne and Mr Bagra up tonight. A fine day.

9th December
1873 Tue: Taking up remainder of the leeks and some brussel sprouts that was laid in. A fine day.

10th December
1873 Wed: Cutting willows that was on the Low Border of the Kitchen Garden and dug them and commenced levelling the celery ridges. A fine day but some wet morning.

11th December
1873 Thu: Wheeling dung on to the asparagus. Clearing of cabbage and wheeling dung onto the globe artichokes. His Lordship left for Innes House today. A fine day.

As explained in Ch 5, Mr Mackie was the Head Gardener at Duff House; he lived with his family in the house near to the gates by Banff Bridge. About 80 years before John Donaldson's time, the Head Gardener was a John Duncan, who married an English lady called Susannah Emmett, they having met at Watton in Hertfordshire before John was Lord Fife's gardener. She wrote letters back to her family and describes their house in 1797 (published in "Souvenir of Sympathy" 1900) as follows:

> *"a neat little house, indeed; prepared in the greatest order for my reception. It stands in the park very near his lordship's house. We have milk and cream from the dairy close by, as the park is open, and with a great many sheep and deer grazing close by our house. One side of the house goes into the garden, the other into the park. There are two bedrooms with two closets each side the chimneys. There is one grate in each chimney. The rooms are wainscoted and painted white. The doors are all painted mahogany colour. There is a pretty grate in the parlour, likewise one in the kitchen, with two closets in each room. We have plenty of coals, wood, and peat for firing. There is a nice pantry and wash-house with shelves and dresser all round."*

The Head Gardener's House being taken down in 1985 to make way for the Co-op

The Canal refers to the canal that was dug in 1732-34 from the back of Duff House to Banff Bay. Most of the carved stones for Duff House were made at William Adam's yard near Queensferry. These were transported to Banff Bay, perhaps on Lord Fife's ships, and then moved to the house on barges along this canal, the seaward end of which was given permission to go through some of the town's land, which at that time extended down to King's Ford. The exact route of the Canal is not known, nor where the Canal Door was that John refers to.

Refer to the note for 19th Dec 1873 about a hurley.

Rev Bruce of Banff (*see note for 30th Oct 1873*) preached about John Ch1 v10: "He was in the world, and the world was made by him, and the world knew him not."

Refer to the note for 29th Nov 1873 about William Craig.

The Kitchen Garden is the area now known as Airlie Gardens.

Innes House *Refer to the note after 31st Dec.*

12th December
1873 Fri: Set fire to the bonfire and made charcoal. Wheeled dung on the New Vinery Border. Put in the rest of the greens. A fine day.

13th December
1873 Sat: Wheeled dung on the celery brake and dug it. A fine day.

14th December
1873 Sun: Travelled about today. Most of the day at Church. In the evening sermon by Mr Bruce from the 10th Chapter of Matthew 28th verse. A fine day.

15th December
1873 Mon: Dunged the cabbage brake and dug it up. At the Ice House in the afternoon with Mr Bagra and the cuddy for ice to go to the Innes House. A fine day.

16th December
1873 Tue: Clearing off the withered leaves from the plants in the morning. Cut some willows at the back of the hotel. Made some shreds. After dinnertime we wheeled on dung on to the leek brake. A very rough rainy morning but it cleared towards evening.

17th December
1873 Wed: Wheeling dung this morning and till after dinnertime that we dug the piece beside the grass. A fine day.

John calls the Airlie Garden Vinery (the only one we know today) the New Vinery. It was only built in 1872. As explained in Chapter 5 there was another Vinery at The Orchard, also growing grapes.

Rev Bruce of Banff (*see note for 30th Oct 1873*) preached about Matthew Ch10 v28: "And fear not them which kill the body, but are not able to kill the soul: but rather fear him which is able to destroy both soul and body in hell."

A cuddy is a donkey, used to pull a cart, in this case laden with ice. The donkey was perhaps an integral part of Duff House, as there is a picture around the turn of the century, of Duff House with a number of early motor cars – and a donkey!

The cuddy is again mentioned 6th Nov 1874, again taking ice from the Ice House. For another source of ice see the note against 13th Jan 1874.

Innes House. *Refer to the note after 31st Dec.*

The Duff House gardens ran along the back of the Fife Arms Hotel on Low St. *See Ch 5 for further information about the garden layout, and the note against 5th Feb 1874 about the hotel.*

Shred. *See the note about Cobb/basket making for 17th Feb.*

18th December

1873 Thu: Digging all day. A row with Mary about the caffy pot. A fine day.

19th December

1873 Fri: Took down a hurleyful of potatoes in the morning. Digging the rest of the day but we was up for another box of ice. William Innes was here today. A fine day.

20th December

1873 Sat: Brought down some holly to the Claytons. Nailing all day. A fine day.

21st December

1873 Sun: Down in the forenoon. Sailing in an old boat hunting waterhens on the island. At Church in the evening, preaching from the 4th Chapter of 2nd Corinthians, the last clause of the 6th verse. A walk with Miss Gray. A fine day. Rough in the evening.

Caffy is coffee. Presumably Mary was the lass that cooked for the gardeners living at the Orchard. There is a Mary Sim, the Head Gamekeepers wife, living in the Gamekeepers Cottage at Duff House, who may well have been doing some housekeeping duties. The Census says she was living at the Gamekeepers Cottage – somewhere close to Duff House based on the Valuation Rolls, potentially the buildings southeast of Duff House.

A hurley, or hurlie, or hurly, is a Victorian wooden wheelbarrow. For light items these would often have additional sides fitted.

William Innes was a gardener at Duff House in 1871. At the time of this visit he would have been 23 years old and therefore presumably working elsewhere, and back for a day visit.

Dr Clayton was the physician to Lord Fife, when he was at home, and therefore presumably worthy of being given a gift at Christmas. He was one of four physicians in Banff at the time. At The Orchard is a really large, hence old, holly tree; perhaps that is where the holly came from.

Dr Clayton and his family lived at 3 High St Banff; it seems this house number did not change when others did later in the 19th century.

There were three sizeable islands in the river; the one with the summerhouse, Scury Island on the bend with the ford, but the largest was Hospital Island below the Mausoleum. Today this is not an island, but it certainly used to be.

Corinthians 2 Ch4 v6: "For God, who commanded the light to shine out of darkness, hath shined in our hearts, to give the light of the knowledge of the glory of God in the face of Jesus Christ."

We are not sure who Miss Gray may have been, she is mentioned only this once, but there was a Hannah Gray, 20 years old in 1873, working as a domestic servant at 4½ Low St, which by coincidence was the same building John's future wife worked in!

22nd December
1873 Mon: Nailing today. A very cold day. Good shower in the afternoon we went into the Vinery and put back the Gladioli roots.

23rd December
1873 Tue: Filled a box of ice to go to Innes House. Nailing till after dinnertime then it came on to snow and we had to stop. I made a bouquet of flowers for Miss Ewen to the ball and cleared snow off the top of the Fruitroom. A bad night.

24th December
1873 Wed: Took down 2 birns of holly, nailed all day. Very cold on the feet, fair above but snow on the ground and bitter.

25th December
1873 Thu: Christmas, we took down two bundles of holly today. Nailing all day. Ingram was over at McDuff for ropeyarn after dinnertime. I was down at the Royal Oak. At my Sean's last night. A fine day today for the nailing, being warm.

26th December
1873 Fri: Some rainy this morning. Cutting shreds and then at the nailing till dinnertime then it came on more and we cut some more shreds and came home about half three o'clock and cleaned out the Vinery. Went to the mill.

Innes House. *Refer to the note after 31ˢᵗ Dec.* It appears Lord Fife and guests spent Christmas 1873 at Innes House.

Nailing was just that; nailing plants to walls so that they grew where you wanted them to. There is a lot of evidence in the brick wall still at The Orchard, as well as the wall to the north of Airlie Gardens, of nailing.

There was an Ann Ewen, 22 years old in 1873, working in Scotstown as a domestic servant. This may or may not have been the Miss Ewen that John made the bouquet for.

The Fruitroom may be referring to The Orchard or the Duff House gardens.

A birn means a bundle; perhaps the holly came from the large tree at The Orchard. On 25ᵗʰ Dec John actually uses the word "bundle".

The rope works were owned by Alexander Carney, listed in Carney St, and his ropes were stretched out, tarred where necessary, along Bankhead ("Ropewalk" on this 1867 map, courtesy of NLS), the seaward side of Low Shore – of course the land now with the shipyard, lifeboat station and Aquarium had not been reclaimed in 1873.

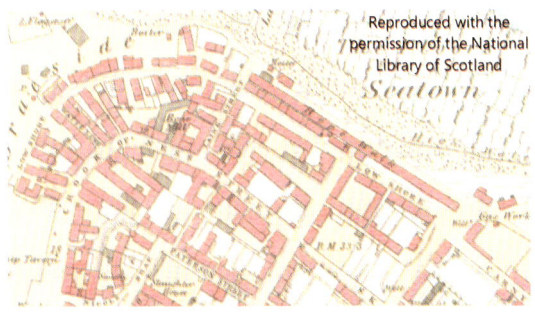

Reproduced with the permission of the National Library of Scotland

Royal Oak – now listed as 10 Bridge St, used to be 5 Bridge St, with the licencee as Mrs Jessie Walker in John Donaldson's time. The Royal Oak in this picture is up on the right where the man is leaning up against the wall (behind the three kids). This was later Barclays Hotel.

We could not trace any Sean in Banff of any surname; he is not mentioned again.

27th December
1873 Sat: Nailing all day but about half an hour before stopping time we took the Spade and after that when we was coming home we cut some evergreens for the Volunteers Hall and went down with them and helped them to busk it and joined the company, Ingram and me. Some showers through the day and very cold.

28th December
1873 Sun: Wasn't at the Church in the forenoon but in the evening and the text was from the 17th Psalm the last verse. After the Church was out I was out a walk with Miss R. A fine day very frosty. Ingram was at Troup.

29th December
1873 Mon: Took down a bundle of holly in the morning. Nailing till dinnertime. Bagra and me went for a box of ice after, after the Spade, pretty cold.

30th December
1873 Tue: Digging for about an hour then nailing the rest of the day about the Canal Door. Was down at the Hall and Bagra joined tonight. A very rough day and very cold.

31st December
1873 Wed: Nailing all day. We got our C.D.V. taken today. Brought in the New Year at the Orchard with some more chaps. Got some tipsy. Went to Banff and had a puruse through it and landed with other three at a place and passed off the morning in the bed with the girls. A fine day, pretty cold.

There were a few hotels listed in Banff, but none as "The Spade". John mentions this – presumably a public house type of thing – three times throughout this Diary. A number of "Spirit Dealers" are listed for Banff:
- John Chalmers, 5 Low Shore
- Mrs M Kinnaird, 11 Boyndie St
- James Mackay, 40 Bridge St
- William Marsden, 3 North Castle St
- Andrew Murray, Old Market Place
- James Watt, North Castle St.

How each of them were known more colloquially is not known.

The Volunteers Hall – ie for the Artillery Volunteers and Rifle Volunteers. Nationally these Corps only started in 1859 and only formed in individual communities once initiated by the Lord Lieutenant of the time. In the 1867 Directory no Volunteers are listed in Banff although official records show the 2nd Banffshire Artillery Volunteer Corps were headquartered at 6 Castle St (where Trend is today), but by 1877 they are listed at the Drill Hall Bridge St. The old Community Centre however was not built until 1925, so the exact location of this initial Drill Hall is not known. *See also note for 1st Jan & 17th Apr 1874.*

On 30th Dec John's fellow gardener, Bagra, also joined the Volunteers.

17th Psalm, last verse: "As for me, I will behold thy face in righteousness: I shall be satisfied, when I awake, with thy likeness."

Troup House. *Refer to the note for 11th Oct 1874.*

Canal Door. *Refer to the note for 6th Dec; & to Chapter 5 for a garden layout.*

A C.D.V. is a Carte de Visite. This was sort of the equivalent to a business card today, but was a photo. There are many of these Victorian CDVs around today, but the annoying thing is that they are generally just photos printed on a card that had been pre-printed with the photographers details, and rarely include the name of the person – unless they write on it!

The photographers in Banff at the time were George Bremner and Rae & Son, both of Bridge St at the time. *See also note for 26th March 1874.*

The "puruse" – perhaps one of John's own words or he may have meant "peruse" – presumably refers to the events related in the Banffie (quoted on the page opposite 1st Jan).

The penultimate phrase of 1873 in John's Diary continues his secretive nature as regards his amorous adventures!

Gardenstown/Gamrie Churches (see 16th Nov '73 and 8th Feb '74)

John makes mention of two churches in Gardenstown, the "New" and the "Free". The history of the various churches can be somewhat confusing and below is an attempt at an outline of the various churches over time:

1/ The old Mohr church, St Johns, built in the 11th century, out on Mohr Head. A storm destroyed the roof in 1827. Services were temporarily held in St John's Manse. The church is now not in use.

2/ What used to be the new Mohr church, Church of Scotland, opened in 1830 over a mile inland to replace the old Mohr church. From about 1850 services were also held in a granary in the village until 4/ was built. It became outside the parish in 1885. The last service was held in 1992. It is now a house. This would have been the "New" church visited by John on 16th Nov 1873.

3/ A United Presbyterian church, built 1847, until it was replaced with 5/. This would have been the "Free" church visited by John 8th Feb 1874.

4/ Church of Scotland built 1875/6 sitting 360 people. At the time this was known as the Mohr church! For a while it had a spire attached. This closed in 1932 and became "The Closed Brethren Hall" which in turn closed about 1980 and it is now a house.

5/ A new United Presbyterian church, built 1898/9. Soon became a United Free church. In 1932 the UP and Church of Scotland congregations merged. The church now calls itself Gardenstown New church.

6/ Free Presbyterian church, built 2004, sited near 2/ above.

Innes House (see 8th Nov, 11th, 15th and 23rd Dec 1873)

Innes House is mentioned four times in the Diary; in all cases taking either onions or ice to it. It had been built in the 1600s, but was another estate owned by the Duffs since 1767, developed a lot by James the 2nd Earl particularly with tree planting. James the 5th Earl, friends and family, spent Christmas in 1873 there. Today the House is run by the Tennant family as a wedding venue, together with 5000 acres of farmland, forest and meadow. It is sited about half way between the village of Urquhart near Llanbryde and the coast.

In the mid-1800s the outside of the main part of Innes House was much as it is today (see second picture), although some gates and balconies have changed. There is no currently known record of any detail of the gardens, although this turn of the century picture shows a little bit.

A modern view from the top of Innes House gives a better idea of the immediate gardens.

1st January
1874 Thu: Got home in the morning and after having some tea put on the Artillery uniform. Was over at the Links, took 3rd prize - 8 shillings and a ham. Albert at the ball in the evening. A fine day some rough for shooting. Towards the end I made out of ground 3 centres, then a bullseye, then an outer, then a bullseye, another outer and the last two, nothing.

2nd January
1874 Fri: Down about half past 12 in the forenoon, dug some but very little. Two loads of trits came today. Melvin away at Gordon Castle. Cold.

3rd January
1874 Sat: Dug some today and nailed some. Melvin came when we was very busy carting down at the artichokes. We got some porter and biscuits and a currant loaf, which he helped us with. Very cold.

From the Banffshire Journal Tue 6th Jan 1874:

NEW YEAR FESTIVITIES IN BANFF

"There was brilliant moonlight on the last evening of the old year, to which was attributable the parading of the streets by bands of young persons. Towards midnight, the fife and drum band of the Artillery Volunteers marched through the town, amusing some, and disturbing others, by strains sometimes not very harmonious. They were accompanied by a crowd, who occasionally gave vent to their feelings by cheering and singing snatches of songs. These proceedings went on till past midnight, and might have continued far into the morning but for the judicious interference of the police. When the band ceased playing, the crowd gradually dispersed. We are informed there has been more drunkenness in Banff, especially among young persons, than at any similar season for six years past."

"At the Links on New Year's Day, the Artillery Corps held their competition. There were 40 members present, and, by the aid of gifts from friends, as many as thirty prizes were offered. The ranges were 100, 200, and 300 yards, three shots at each. The highest score made was 28."

The Banffie only gives the names of the winner and runner up, so John, 3rd prize, doesn't quite get mentioned!

We cannot fully identify or understand this word, possibly "trits".

Gordon Castle was a lot more extensive than it is today. *See also note for 20th Jul.*

Porter was a beer that had a high hop content and was dark in colour, with a typical alcohol content of 6.6% by volume (modern beers are circa 3.5% to 5%). During the nineteenth century it was confused with the word "stout" and was used interchangeably.

4th January
1874 Sun: Down in the afternoon. Went to the brewery saw my uncle; went home with him, got my tea. They were at me about being a father. Was at the Church, the text was in the 26th chapter of Acts 27th verse. Miss R came home yesterday. Very frosty when the Church came out and cold.

5th January
1874 Mon: Down at digging the piece before the Little Vinery. Commenced the Long Border today. Cold and strong frost in the morning; the roads like glass

6th January
1874 Tue: Near half an hour late this morning. Nailing all day. A fine day. Got a letter from Kingshorn.

7th January
1874 Wed: Digging a small piece beside the Canal Door and nailing the rest of the day. Up in the evening to Boyndie Road, Bagra and me, but nothing happened. A fine day, some rough.

8th January
1874 Thu: Nailing all day. Killed a pig. To Mr Mackie in the afternoon. Got our pay today I got £5 and 8 shillings this time. A cold rough day.

9th January
1874 Fri: Finished the nailing at Mackies today. Dug up the artichokes. Splendid day.

10th January
1874 Sat: Dug over the artichokes a second time for any that we had missed. Wheeled on dung on the border from the artichokes. To Mackies and dug a piece beside the Canal door. Cold. Went up in the evening to Boyndie Road. Took with the changes.

The Banff Brewery, started in the 18th century, was at 83 Castle St, where Meadowlands and other businesses are today.

Not to be confused with the Distillery that used to be at Boyndie.

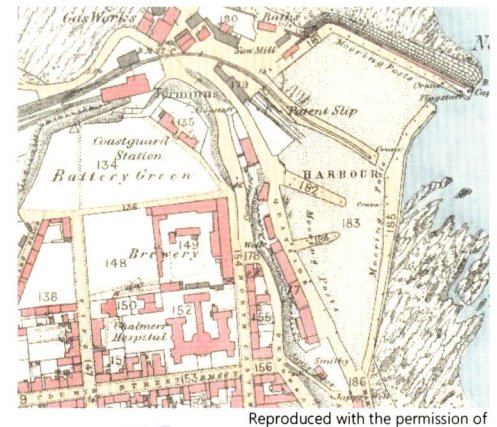

Reproduced with the permission of the National Library of Scotland

The reference to being a father is explained in Ch 2. See also 10th & 27th Feb.

Acts Ch26 v27:

The Little Vinery presumably refers to the one at the Orchard.

See note for 6th Dec 1873 for the Canal Door.

£5 8 shillings (£5.40) was John's salary per quarter. Over the year (see also 1st April, 2nd July & 1st Oct) John earned £22 6s for the year. With inflation that equates to £33,000 in 2022, so not a bad salary! As this was his standard pay for a quarter it seems likely he actually started work on 1st Oct 1873, four weeks before the Diary itself starts.

There was a liquor dealer at 11 Boyndie St and it may be this establishment that John went to. Today, this is the Town and County Club. Originally the building had been built by George Robinson in 1772; he was principally a linen manufacturer, at one time employing up to 2,400 people locally, linen being one of the main items sent south from Banff. After 1825 there is no recorded history but perhaps it fits being a "pub" in 1874, the licencees being Mr and Mrs Kinnaird.

11th January
1874 Sun: Rose about 12 o'clock. Pyper and Wiseman up in the afternoon, went down to town with them. Was not at Church today. Came up to the Orchard with a girl and spent the evening. Cold.

12th January
1874 Mon: Digging the most of the day but sometimes when it was snowing awful picked the neth leaves from the plants. Terrible cold, snowing most of the day.

13th January
1874 Tue: Digging this forenoon. About 3 inches of snow on the ground today. Up at the Turners for the Russian Muscat. Rolling snow an hour after dinnertime and then went to the Spade for a few minutes then to the Hill of Down for ice. A fine day above.

14th January
1874 Wed: Digging all day. Nearly finished the Long Border today. Lord Fife came here yesterday. A fine day.

15th January
1874 Thu: At the Orchard today cutting willows all day. A fine day.

16th January
1874 Fri: At the Orchard pruning gooseberries all day. Very soft and cold.

17th January
1874 Sat: At the Orchard in the morning pruning. Went down and wheeled on dung to the strawberries before dinnertime and then went up to the Plantation for stakes in the afternoon. A fine day, some cold.

The word "neth" is not all clear but the meaning is probably clear, the dead or naff leaves.

As it is the middle of the working day, notwithstanding John did pop into the "Spade"! the reference to Russian Muscat is presumably to vines, not wine. However we have not been able to identify any vine growers or even nurserymen called Turner.

In the nineteenth century at the time of John Donaldson, at the top of the Hill of Down (the old name for Macduff before 1783), now more often called Doune Hill, there used to be two small lochans, the larger called Star Loch.

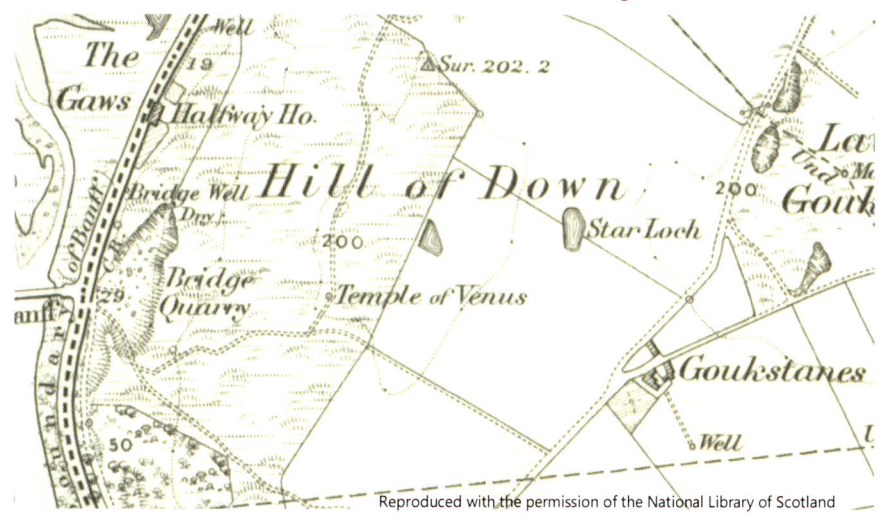

Reproduced with the permission of the National Library of Scotland

Being higher, and still, shallow water, these are likely to freeze well before the River Deveron does, and hence a good place to collect ice. The day before John refers to being "terrible cold". The Temple of Venus had been standing for 130 years or so by this time; Goukstanes is where Dounemount Care Home is today. See also 13th and 14th Feb 1874 when ice was taken from the river.

Lord Fife was visiting Duff House with a friend, the Honourable Hamilton Duncan.

The Plantation may have referred to the Sandyhill or Colleonard Nurseries, the other side of the Aberchirder Road to The Orchard, but outside the Duff estate. This had long been in existence as mostly a tree nursery.

18th January
1874 Sun: Up at about 11 o'clock went down to Banff about 3 p.m. Met Mr Pyper and Mr Wiseman went round by "The Foresters" and through the wood of Montcoffer and round by the Bridge of Alvah in the afternoon. At Church in the evening. A strange minister preached from the 1st Chapter of Second Timothy 10th verse. After Church came out there was a ship in the bay in danger. So we went over to the boathouse and the crowd took over the lifeboat to Banff harbour and took the crew off, very rough night but a land wind.

19th January
1874 Mon: Went down in the morning, spread dung on the strawberries. Went up and nibbed out our stakes at the Plantation and then pruning redcurrants at the Orchard. Commenced to stake out some rows between them before night. Fine day, cold.

20th January
1874 Tue: Took out the rest of the bushes. Pruned the blackcurrants today. Took out the row of gooseberries that was above the Vinery. Mackay was up today. A fine day, some cold.

21st January
1874 Wed: Commenced to trench the border at the Beech Hedge. Trenched all day. Fine day.

22nd January
1874 Thu: Trenching all day. Finished the border tonight. A splendid day.

The Foresters sounds like a pub, but which one is not known. The walk around Montcoffer and the Bridge of Alvah is a few miles, and presumably quite bracing.

Timothy2 Ch1 v10: "But is now made manifest by the appearing of our Saviour Jesus Christ, who hath abolished death, and hath brought life and immortality to light through the gospel."

The **ship in the bay** in danger was the 132 ton brig, the "Essex". She had left Sunderland about a month previously with a cargo of coal for Mr William Watson (14 Castle St), merchant in Banff. Her voyage had been tortuous anyway, having to take shelter at Holy Island from previous storms. She had then made Wick, but needed some repairs. She had sailed the day before and made Portsoy and took on a pilot to help her get to Banff, where she arrived at about 5pm and anchored in Banff Bay. With the violent northwest storm carrying away her topsail sheets, she became unmanageable and the crew became alarmed, setting off rockets.

The **lifeboat** was at that time housed just on the Macduff side of the bridge. The Banffshire Journal carries on with the story:

"Horses kindly furnished by Mr Frank Wood of Banff Brewery hauled the boat as far as Bridge Street, when they were unloosed, and the crowd who had gathered hauled the boat up Bridge Street, along Low Street, down Carmelite St and along the shore to Banff Harbour. This long route was adopted in order to avoid the narrow and abrupt turnings by Old Market Place. The boat was launched, and soon amidst cheers from the assembled crowd, sped out of the harbour towards the vessel. The lifeboat, from the heavy rolling of the ship, had to thrown the anchor, and drop down upon the vessel. The crew were transferred with considerable difficulty. On account of the force and direction of the wind, after shipping several seas, the lifeboat gave up the endeavour to return to Banff, and bore up and made for Macduff. There the crew of the Essex were cared for…" "The Essex was left riding at anchor in the bay, and at daybreak, was found to have ridden out the storm." The crew reboarded and she got safely into Macduff.

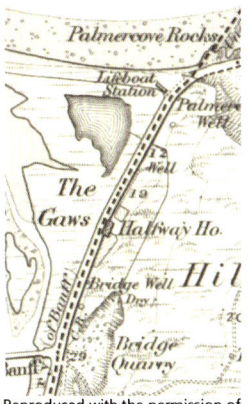

Reproduced with the permission of the National Library of Scotland

23rd January
1874 Fri: Digging all forenoon. Got away at dinnertime - a half holiday in honour of the Duke of Edinburgh's Marriage. I was down on the Green Banks firing a feu du joie with the Artillerymen. Collected in the Hall after 6 o'clock and had a spree and dancing. A few fireworks in the town. Went home to my bed about 1 o'clock a.m. A fine day.

24th January
1874 Sat: At the Orchard digging all day in the Upper Garden but at intervals when showers of snow came we went to bark the vines. A very stormy day, the ground white.

25th January
1874 Sun: Rose about 2 o'clock p.m. At Church a strange minister tonight. Text was Second Timothy 4th Chapter, verse 6. A fine day. Awful ice and dubs.

26th January
1874 Mon: At the Orchard digging all day in the Upper Garden. A fine day, rough towards evening.

27th January
1874 Tue: At the Orchard digging all day. A fine day.

28th January
1874 Wed: At the Orchard digging all day. A most splendid day. Mr Mackie was up this afternoon administering a dose of something to the vines.

29th January
1874 Thu: At the Orchard today. Finished the Upper Half digging. Dug 2 brakes in the Lower Half. Shot a she bullfinch at dinner time. A fine day.

30th January
1874 Fri: Commenced the Lower Garden. A most splendid day.

The Duke of Edinburgh was Alfred, the fourth child of Queen Victoria and Prince Albert. He married the Grand Duchess Maria, the only surviving daughter of Alexander II, the Czar of Russia. The event took place in St Petersburg, "with imperial splendour, and no court in Europe can match the full pomp of the Winter Palace" according to The Times.

A feu de joie is a salute fired by soldiers, each firing in succession along the ranks to make a continuous sound.

Timothy2 Ch4 v6: "For I am now ready to be offered, and the time of my departure is at hand."

Dubs means mud.

"a dose of something" in the care of vines. *Refer to the "Grape Growing" note next to 26th Oct 1874.*

Bullfinch. *See note for 31st Jan.*

31st January
1874 Sat: Finished the Orchard digging today. Was working in the Lower Garden yesterday all day although I forgot last night's writing. We have been two days and a half in the Lower Garden. My she bullfinch died yesterday morning. So it is all dug but the Willow Border and all the edges of the brakes, the Vinery Border and round the outside of the Vinery Hedge and our Flower Garden and some odds and ends. A fine day again.

1st February
1874 Sun: James Bagra came up with us last night to sleep so we had him here this morning and as I was dressing my brother came in at the door so we went away down to the waterside, took the boat and had some sport. Then we came home and the Foreman and Mr Bagra joined us to dinner. Then we went down to the other Bothy and then came home again to let James Webster away. So I went away a piece with him so I was not at Church today. He took away the fiddle with him. Splendid day.

2nd February
1874 Mon: Down at the other garden today. We had J Bagra last night again. He went home today. We dug the end of the Long Border at Mackie's House today, took up the yellow pyrethrum and put it in at the corner of the dyke. Clearing the trellice of the Flower Garden, pruning roses etc. Clearing the border and the places for the apricot trees etc. A splendid day.

3rd February
1874 Tue: Clipping the hedge in the bottom of the garden today. Clearing the half of the onion bed pulling out the onions that was growing through the weeds. Digging the border from that to the horse-radish. A fine day.

4th February
1874 Wed: Wheeling dung to the trenched piece beside the Little Vinery for a short time this morning. Washing the wall with hot water the rest of the day. A fine day.

Bullfinches are not common birds in the wild today. People keeping birds as pets (as mentioned by John later on in the Diary) or eating various wild birds as was common in the nineteenth century, must have caused a reduction in the number of wild birds.

Thomas Edward, the Banff naturalist was alive and working in Banff during the course of John's Diary.

Thomas advises it was common to keep a bird caged for it's beauty, and in particular the bullfinch because it was "easily taught to whistle or "pipe" familiar tunes".

John had shot this bullfinch just two days previously so it's chances of survival were probably slim!

This image of a hand coloured print of a male bullfinch is from the "*Feathered Tribes of the British Islands*" by Robert Mudie, dated 1841.

For the first time John refers to the Orchard garden as "our", almost a competitive feeling to the expression against the "other" garden in Banff.

Washing the walls of a Vinery with hot water is part of the care of vines. *Refer to the note on the page for 26th Oct 1874.*

5th February

1874 Thu: Digging the trenched border that we levelled yesterday down at the Little Vinery. Took out brussel sprouts out of the border at the back of the hotel. Dunged and dug it. Dug the horse-radish. Commenced to chop down the fale up in the wood for the Vinery Border. A fine day.

6th February

1874 Fri: Chopping some fale for the inside of the Vinery all day. Fine.

7th February

1874 Sat: Chopping some more fale in the morning and then drawing some marks to plant kale in but it come on rain and we was forced to leave it and go to the House. Went to the Vinery cleaned some bark off the vines. Went to Troup with William Bagra in the afternoon. Was down between 4 and 5. Got a very bad night going down. We was wet to the skin on one side.

8th February

1874 Sun: At Troup today; a very stormy morning. Went down to the gardens and down to the seaside. Very rough and cold. After dinner went out for a while and then came in to tea after which we came home. Stopped at the Free Church till the folk was in and then James Bagra and Grey came down the road with us a bit. Home before 8 o'clock.

9th February

1874 Mon: We was working this forenoon at little or anything - some miscellaneous jobs. After dinner took down willows and made them ready for boiling. A cold rough day.

10th February

1874 Tue: Down in the morning got the boiler in order, and had 4 boils of willows and skinned them today. Got word that I had become a father last night. A fine frosty day.

The Fife Arms Hotel on Low Street was built by the Duffs and completed in 1845. Duff House at this time was short of bedrooms as the wings on the House had never been built, and the hotel provided the ability to have multiple guests and at the same time be a self-sustaining commercial enterprise.

In 1868 it was described as "there is not a more commodious and comfortable [hotel] north of Edinburgh"; "with every elegance and comfort that money can procure, capital stabling for horses, and conveyances of every description at command."

It was built on the site of the Black Bull Inn on Low Street, where Dr Samuel Johnson and James Boswell visited in 1773, as was recorded in Johnson's Diary and Boswell's biography of him.

The Earl Fifes obviously used it themselves from time to time because in 1888 a visitor wrote in her published diary:

"It was easy to see what they thought of us at the Fife Arms, where we stayed in Banff. We were given our breakfast with the nurse and children, while the great man breakfasted in state in a near dining-room. They ate very like ordinary children, but their clothes showed them to be little boys and girls of aesthetic distinction. I fear, however, we were not properly impressed."

The hotel later became a Trust House hotel and took over part of the garden behind where John Donaldson used to work – *see Chapter 5*.

Fale. "Fale" or "Fail" means a cut piece of turf. In this case it is used upside down on top of the drains round the outside and inside of the Vinery, and then buried in the soil. *Refer to the note on Grape growing opposite 26th Oct 1874.*

Troup. *Refer to the note for 10th Oct 1874.*

Gardenstown Free Church. *Refer to the note after 31st Dec 1873.*

Making willows ready for boiling. *Refer to the note against cobbs/making baskets for 17th Feb 1874.*

Being a father is explained in Ch 2. See also *4th Jan, 27th Feb and 7th Apr.*

11th February

1874 Wed: Wheeling dung on to the border in the Flower Garden and to the spinach neuk beside the Door and dug it. Bagra and me was riddling ashes till dinnertime and the other two was up in the wood riddling mould after dinner. Bagra and me went to the plantation and filled the stakes that we took out. There was one cart doing them. The other two was riddling the rest of the ashes. 9 degrees of frost this morning but a fine day above.

12th February

1874 Thu: Throwing up the vegetable hillock in the wood and down at the Fruitroom the hillock there. Mackie came up and told us about the election in Morayshire that was the day before for a Member of Parliament between Lord Macduff and Lord Reidhaven, Macduff had a majority of 210. Bagra and me went to the wood of Montcoffer for birch and the other two up to the Laundry for a hurleyful of spruce branches to cover some of the tender plants in the Flower Garden. In the afternoon Bagra and me was put up to clean out the Ice House to get in ice tomorrow. A fine day but frosty last night again.

13th February

1874 Fri: In the forenoon was sawing and pointing stakes for the strawberries. At the Ice House in the afternoon filling it out of Deveron beside the bridge. A fine day but very frosty last night.

14th February

1874 Sat: Down to the Ice House in the morning filled this one here in the forenoon. In the afternoon was down at the new one we about half filled one of the ends of it and stopped before 2 o'clock for want of ice. A fine day. Not frosty last night.

15th February

1874 Sun: Rose today between 9 and 10 o'clock. Got an old catapult and I was going about. Bagra and Little Wiseman came up and we went down to the boat beneath the House. I killed a waterhen which Wiseman took to get stuffed. Going home, Ingram and me plundered the laundry. Pyper and Mr Wiseman was up in the afternoon so went down the walks pinning birds. At Church in the evening, Mr Bruce preaching First Hebrews 3rd Chapter, 19th verse. A fine day.

Mould is the word for "compost".

Lord Macduff was Viscount Macduff, the oldest son of the 5th Earl Fife; Lord Reidhaven was Viscount Reidhaven, the oldest – the only in this case - son of the 7th Earl of Seafield.

Viscount Reidhaven was a Conservative and Viscount Macduff a Liberal.

From 1841 to 1874 the Liberal's had had the majority in parliament – but 1874 saw William Gladstone lose, and Benjamin Disraeli's Conservatives win a significant majority of MPs – meaning Viscount Macduff was part of the Opposition. It was noteable however that the Liberal's had overall more votes across the country, but had been unable to field candidates in many constituencies so those Conservative candidates were elected unopposed.

The elected MP for Banff that year (and before and after) was Sir William Robert Duff – also a Liberal.

See note for 19th Feb 1874 about the Ice House. The main Duff House Ice House is a buried egg shaped design, not far from The Orchard. But we don't know where the "new one" was; clearly it was a different design as it had ends. The ice for this came from the River Deveron; the last few days had been very frosty as John records. There is a well known local photo of people walking and curling on the river by Banff Bridge. A month earlier ice had come from the top of Doune Hill (*see note for 13th Jan 1874*).

Pinning is a term for shooting or hitting with a stone. Shooting birds is a reasonably common activity for John, see 10th and 11th Mar and 10th July, with notes.

Hebrews Ch3 v19: "So we see that they could not enter in because of unbelief."

16th February
1874 Mon: Sawing and pointing the stakes that we left on Friday. Hacking the ends for firewood and shimming some of them. Among them all day. A fine day.

17th February
1874 Tue: Commenced the baskets. Splitting some old ash in the afternoon. Bagra and me was over at Montcoffer for old willows to make cobbs. A fine day in the afternoon, raining forenoon. Shearer's mare fell.

18th February
1874 Wed: At the baskets all day. Today at the soiree in the parish Church in the evening but I might as well have stopped at home for it was not worth much. A find day but frosty. Got milk from Jane Downie tonight, for the first time on the 18th January. Last night being Bannock Night I was away with some more out in the country, landed at Wardine. Had some dancing and very few bannocks.

A cobb is a basket, in this case made of willow. The various stages of preparing for this are as follows:

Cutting the shreds: see 16th Dec 1873 and 15th Jan 1874. The gardeners also collect some "old willows" on 17th Feb from Montcoffer – presumably that the farm there had collected. Tradition has it that willows should be cut between Michaelmas (around the end of September) and Candlemas (2nd February).

Boiling the shreds: on 10th Dec 1873 John did 4 boilings, and on 12th Mar 1874 he did some more. It only takes a few hours of boiling to soften the willow, but it has a further benefit of making the colour more even and deeper.

Mellowing: which John does not refer to. This is wrapping them in damp cloths to keep them soft and pliable. Care must be taken not to let them go mouldy. One way to check there has been enough boiling is to bend the shred at right angles across say the end of your thumb, and it must not crack on the outside.

Weaving: this is a job for bad weather days, which quite often is what John and his fellow gardeners apparently do. John's Diary makes reference on 8 days for making baskets, often all day (see Feb 17th-20th; 26th & 27th, also 13th & 14th Mar 1874).

Using the baskets: the amount of effort in making baskets may seem a lot, but John makes 21 later references to sending baskets of all sorts of things, both to Duff House but also to other people, often several baskets at once. Apples (many sorts), plums, damsons, black and red currants, gooseberries, also onions and carrots.

The name Shearer was common in Banff in the 1870's, families of at least George (a tailor), Solomon, John and James (a baker).

Jane Downie (age 49 at the time of the Diary) was the Dairy Maid at Duff House, living in the House itself.

Bannock Night is the Scottish version of Shrove Tuesday. A Bannock is pan fried bread, perhaps made traditionally with oats or barley. Originally fried on a Bannock stone. It seems there are many many different recipes, and can be served with a whole variety of accompaniments, or of course themselves accompanying a main meal. We have not been able to identify "Wardine" where John had his few bannocks.

19th February
1874 Thu: Basket making today again all day. Bagra and Ingram was up at the Ice House in the afternoon putting in some straw before the masons would build up the doors. Fine day frost in the morning.

20th February
1874 Fri: Basket making today again. We would have been mixing the mould for the vinery today. It was raining like in the morning so it was postponed. It was raining in the afternoon. Finished my basket all but cutting the ends.

21st February
1874 Sat: Mixing bones and dung through the hillock for this and hoeing it this afternoon. A fine day.

22nd February
1874 Sun: Ranging about through the woods and in the boat the most of the day. Was going to the Church in the evening but turned at the door and went down to the boat. A fine day.

23rd February
1874 Mon: Commenced today The Changing of the Hours. Digging in the morning before the Vinery. At the Orchard down at 11 o'clock. Laying pipes in the New Vinery Border and pinting over the surface of it with forks and preparing hillocks for the vegetable marrows. Threw up some dung for the hot bed and filled in the tracks of the road past the Fruitroom. See till six o'clock now. A fine day.

24th February
1874 Tue: Digging before the Vinery in the morning. After breakfast dunged and dug a brake all but a bit for the celery; we did not dig it. Took a Hawk when I came home. A very cold but dry day.

Based on John's notes in the Diary it seems the Ice House was closed up in the summer – "the masons building up the doors". It is not until 30th Oct that the Ice House is opened up again.

The present design of the Ice House seems as though it used to have a double airlock, ie three doors to get in; but whether these were all in place in 1874 is not known; on any maps it is just shown as a rectangle. Obviously the open grille that is on the top of the Ice House today was not there when it was in operation, and all of it would have been covered with considerably more soil than it is today, acting as insulation. It is possible that in fact there was an original opening in the top, so that ice and food could be lowered down and up, and then the opening filled with some sort of bung, but John makes no mention of this.

The Ice House was filled with food and ice, with different foods separated by columns and layers of straw. With the drain in the bottom, any melting ice would drain away and not freeze everything into a solid block. The Head Gardener then kept a plan of what was in the Ice House so that the Cook could get what she asked for!

The Duff House Ice House is as good a one as almost anywhere, matching others for size and made of red brick so it has a nice smooth and domed internal lining. On 19th February John's two fellow gardeners were presumably putting a large layer of straw on top to give maximum insulation before the summer.

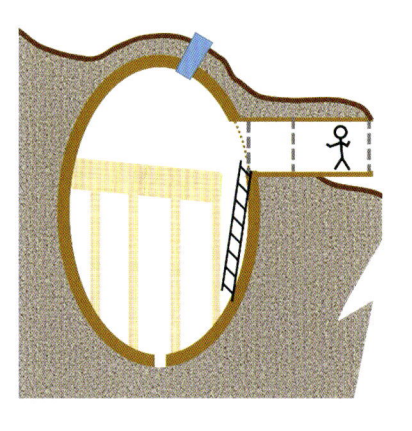

As for 17th Nov, the Changing of the Hours refers to the gardeners working hours.

The Fruitroom was the corner castellated building, still existing, in Airlie Gardens. *See Chapter 5 for a garden layout.*

"Pinting" can be filling in holes (according to the Dialect of Banffshire in 1866), but more generally pointing or smoothing.

Refer to the note against 28th Feb about the Hawk.

25th February

1874 Wed: Took down potatoes this morning, clearing off the cabbages etc from the brake beside the Fruitroom. Dung and dug it. Sowed peas and beans and some onions today for the first, over in the border on the north side of the Kitchen Garden. Got home the apricot trees tonight. Commenced forcing one of the New Vineries last Monday 23rd (I forgot to enter it in here at the time). A very cold rough day but dry.

26th February

1874 Thu: A very cold rough morning so we did nothing this morning. At the Orchard after breakfast we took in some leaf mould to the shed and was at the baskets the rest of the day. A awful bad day, a south east storm.

27th February

1874 Fri: Did nothing at the Orchard today, the ground was too wet. Making baskets all day. A very rainy day, dried some in the afternoon. Was down at the Registrar Office tonight.

28th February

1874 Sat: Dug a short time at the Orchard. Commenced to build a house for the Hawk and the Owl after breakfast. Planted the apricots and some pear trees that came along with them then nailed them, Planted the gooseberries that came at the Orchard in the Peach Border. A splendid day.

1st March

1874 Sun: Up early today down for the milk after breakfast. Up to the Bridge of Alvah. Had a terrible time with a squirl, hunted it a long time but did not get it. Was not at Church today. Pretty cold.

2nd March

1874 Mon: Dug some in the morning. Watered the new Vinery. Today commenced forcing the other house. A little nailing the apricots and putting up a hotbed frame. Bagra was up today; he came on Saturday. A mild day.

The awful bad day on Thursday 26th Feb 1874 seems to have been really quite bad. The Banffie reports "The storm has been disastrous to shipping on the north-east coast."
In Banff a good many houses had dislodged tiles, and the force of the driven rain "found the slightest opening and did harm to the interior."
The Stonehaven lifeboat was launched for a ship in distress, but it carried on northwards. The lifeboat was unable to get back into Stonehaven so made for Aberdeen; just as it was going into the new harbour breakwaters it was engulfed by a wave and then wrecked; four lifeboatmen lost their lives.
Several other ships were wrecked or beached and several seamen lost their lives.
Three days later a schooner – the "Charlotte" - appeared off Macduff in a very disabled state, with boats stove in, bulwarks smashed and generally in a poor state. A seaman and the ships dog had been swept overboard. It was on passage to Aberdeen with a cargo of china clay.

The Registrar's Office was at 4 Low Street Banff. John attended to register the birth of his daughter on 9th Feb 1874; he is named as the father on the birth certificate, and his daughter was named as Isabella Donaldson. John did not seem to be in an ongoing relationship with her mother, who, as explained in Chapter 2, went on to marry and move away from Banff. See also 4th Jan and 10th Feb 1874. She was baptised on 7th April.

John had managed to catch a hawk on 24th Feb; he hasn't mentioned when he managed to catch the owl. He presumably was quite taken with the birds, making the effort to build a cage for the birds. However he released the hawk on 9th March. No further mention is made of the owl.
John had previously kept a "she bullfinch", after having shot it!, although that died two days later (see 29th & 31st Jan 1874).

The Bridge of Alvah had been built by the 2nd Lord Fife in 1772 – when there was no Banff Bridge (first one collapsed in 1768, the present one built in 1779) as a means of more easily getting to Aberdeen and onwards to London where he sat in the House of Lords.

John hunts squirrels a number of times in the Diary, sometimes successfully. This would have been a red squirrel; greys were only imported from the 1890s. This is the only time he spells the word "squirl", presumably just by what the word sounds like.

We have been unable to identify any other information about who Bagra was.

3rd March
1874 Tue: Digging the border down the side of the trilace of the flower garden. A mild day. Planting cabbages in the afternoon. A fine day. A cattle show in Banff today. At the Sishon tonight.

4th March
1874 Wed: Picking out the nails of the Peach Wall. At the Orchard this morning levelling the Strawberry Brake that was trenched in the end of the year. Dug and dunged it. Filling up blanks among the oldest Brake of strawberries. Sent away Willows to Robert Ewen. A fine day. The new Gooseberries that came from R Smith type Ludimar Worcester were thumpers. London. Telegraph. Careless. Stockwell. Leveller. Dan's Mistake. Drill. Conquering Hero. Shiner. Antagonist.

5th March
1874 Thu: Digging and nailing the new Gooseberries in the morning. Made up the Celery Ridges in the forenoon. Preparing the edges around the Shoe for new Boxwood to be laid in the afternoon. A fine day.

6th March
1874 Fri: Prepared the edges and laid Box today around the Shoe. A fine day.

7th March
1874 Sat: Finished the Box laying round the Shoe this morning. Watered the latest Vinery. Prepared and laid in the Cerastium round the Shoe. Mr Mackie and Ingram was sowing the first of the seeds for the Hotbed this afternoon.

8th March
1874 Sun: James Bagra was up in the morning so we went away up the walks. Let away my hawk today. Not at church today. Rainy day.

Trilace is assumed to mean trellis, in the flower garden to support some flowers. This is only the second time (see 2nd Feb when it was cleaned) the Flower Garden trellis is referred to. John uses two different spellings; Trellice and Trilace; a rare example when John didn't correct his own spelling.

The United Banffshire Agricultural Society Spring Show was held on the Tuesday, and reported as an excellent cattle show and more. Duff House Home Farm entered a pair of three year old polled heifers, called "Lady Love" and "Beauty" – they won their class – they were also the only entries! Duff House also won the two year old polled Heifer class against competition!
The Earl of Fife purchased the prize winning peas from the show; this is relevant as John records he was planting peas by 25th March.

We don't know where the Sishon was. *See also 7th Apr.*

The word "brake" is a general word for a garden bed that has a concentration of one sort of plant; in this case strawberries.

Robert Ewen appears three times in the Diary; John also meets him in Edinburgh. The only Robert Ewen in the 1871 Census was the son of Jane or Janet Ewen who ran a laundry in Seafield St, Whitehills. His occupation is listed as "Mariner" at 37 years old so it doesn't really fit to be sending him some Willows, be that plants or shreds. On 11th Nov 1874 John and Robert visited a large Edinburgh Nursery, and Robert then went on to Thirlestane Castle, Lauder in the Borders, presumably where he was a gardener.

John rarely lists varieties of a vegetable or fruit, but for the gooseberry he lists eleven varieties. This may be indicative of the craze that there was in the mid-nineteenth century for gooseberries. There were several hundred Gooseberry Shows annually throughout the year, with many growers competing in various categories. Of the 11 named by John we have tracked down four that are still available from specialist fruit nurseries. The Gooseberry Ludimar Worcester that John calls "thumpers" was a variety that we could not find. *See note for 1st June.*

"Shoe" refers to the Horseshoe shaped bed, a major feature of Airlie Garden.

John had captured the hawk on 24th Feb – see note for 28th Feb.

9th March
1874 Mon: A very stormy day. Making labels in the forenoon. Taking off Verbena cuttings and putting them into pots in the afternoon. Ground white. Rough stormy day.

10th March
1874 Tue: Two or three inch of snow all over today. Putting in the rest of the Verbena cuttings. Put in Salvia, and Linarias [Linicia] and Gazania [Gasinia] and made labels and had fine sport killing blackbirds. Cold stormy day and more snow tonight.

11th March
1874 Wed: A stormy day. More than half a foot of snow on the ground. Put in some cuttings of Allyssum and covered the Apricots in the afternoon. Shooting blackbirds and maraces most of the day.

12th March
1874 Thu: Preparing Willows for a boil in the forenoon and boiled them in the afternoon. A fine day above snow not all away.

13th March
1874 Fri: Up at Miss Brough's garden helping John Clark to prune the wall trees. The rest of them were making baskets. A fine day but some showers.

14th March
1874 Sat: Making baskets today. Raining mostly all day. Down at Mr Mackies last night learning to make murlins.

Three times John refers to shooting blackbirds, these two days and 10th July 1874. Being brought up in the country it would seem unlikely he doesn't know the different types of birds, but as a gardener blackbirds are not generally too much of a problem bird; crows and rooks however are likely to be more of an issue. So it is unclear if John really means blackbirds, or the larger black birds such as rooks, crows, magpies and jackdaws. He spells it as one word, but writes "Blackburds" or "Blburds" in March, and spells it correctly in July.

Birds were quite often used in pies, not only game birds but crows, larks, buntings and fieldfares were not uncommon. The meat would be taken off the crows and larger birds first, by cutting or boiling, but larks would be eaten bones and all (after plucking and removal of head – normally – and legs). We could only find one recipe (published in 1888 – see picture) for actually eating blackbirds in a pie; nothing in the collection of recipes in the library in Duff House (although there is one for Larks en Ragout!).

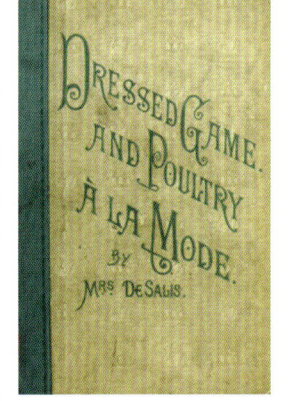

It seems unlikely that John would be shooting small birds for eating – they generally would be caught in nets so that the shot pellets did not making eating difficult.

The word "maraces" is unclear as to what John means; whether some form of bird or another animal.

There is of course the well known rhyme, "four and twenty blackbirds, baked in a pie ….". However lots of sources make it clear that this was based on the practice of wanting to make a show at dinner parties, to make yours memorable compared to your neighbours. A pie crust, bottom, sides and top, would be baked, and a hole put in the bottom; live blackbirds would be put inside the crust, with the surprise that as the host cut into the pie, the blackbirds would fly out!

Refer to the note for 17th Feb 1874 about boiling willows.

We have been unable to identify Miss Brough or what John meant by "murlins".

15th March
1874 Sun: Not anything of importance today but hen broth at dinner. Was not at church today. Had a walk out the Gaveney Brae after church came out at eight. Pretty dull day, raining sometimes.

16th March
1874 Mon: Weeding Daisies in the forenoon. J Melvine and me was shifting Geraniums in the afternoon, Little Davy and Trentham Rose. The other two was weeding. A fine mild day.

17th March
1874 Tue: Digging in the morning. Shifting Geraniums today. Bijou and Stella, all the bedding kinds shifted today and some cuttings of Fuchsias potted. Filled a bag of mould for Miss Stephen. Miss D was up today. A fine day.

18th March
1874 Wed: Took down a hurlieful of potatoes this morning. Shifted all that is in the new Vinery, ferns and all. Gave my plant the name of Shah. A fine day but colder by nearly twenty degrees than two days before.

19th March
1874 Thu: Digging in the morning. Shifting plants all day. All the cactuses today and geraniums and everything clean along. Rained all forenoon from breakfast time; very rough in the afternoon.

20th March
1874 Fri: Raining in the morning. Shifting plants all day. They are all shifted but some down in the little Vinery. Put away a bag of mould to Miss Stephen.

21st March
1874 Sat: Shifted the last of the plants today. Washing the tables in the new Vinery in the afternoon and watering the plants. A fine day.

Gaveney Brae today goes through the middle of the Distillery, but this was only built 1960-62. Before the building of the main road – the A947 – along the Howe of Gellymill was built, it used to be the main road to Aberdeen. This can be seen on the first Scottish road map of 1792 (Taylor & Skinner). NB This also shows that the track through the Duff House estate over the Bridge of Alvah was also a main route. *See also photo opposite 8th June.*

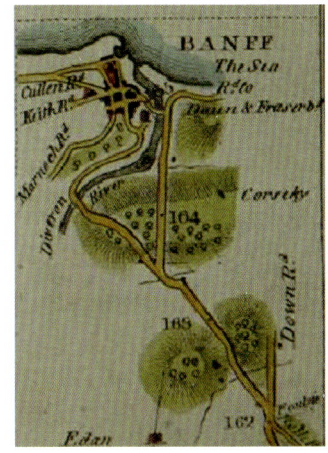

Trentham Rose. *See note for 12th Nov 1873.*

"Little Davy" may be "Little David" Geranium (photo); there is quite a lot of modern reference to it, and one reference was found in 1874, alongside the silver edged Geranium "Bijou", in the Loughcrew Garden planting plans in Ireland. "Stella" Geraniums were also found in references in the mid-1800s.

"Stephen" was a very popular surname in Banff and Banffshire; we don't know who John was referring to. Mould means compost – perhaps leaf mould. The bag was sent to her on 20th March. *See also 11th Oct 1874.*

Perhaps John had a sentimental side to him, naming a plant! Shah can't have been a common name; perhaps it was named after Shah Nasser al-Din, the first Shah of Persia (modern day Iran) to have visited – and made a Knight of the Order of the Garter by Queen Elizabeth, and hence had been in the news – perhaps demonstrating John used to read the Banffshire Journal at least.

The little Vinery is assumed to be the Vinery at The Orchard; the new Vinery is the large one in Airlie Gardens.

22nd March
1874 Sun: Didn't get up today till about 1 o'clock so that we got dinner and breakfast all together and got a shave and down to the town. Was not at church today. A fine day.

23rd March
1874 Mon: Digging in the morning. After breakfast we limed the seed pit at the Fruitroom and took all in to the shed but Patterson's and the Golds. After dinner took soot up to the onion brake at the Orchard, broke it in and put on the soot. A fine day.

24th March
1874 Tue: Digging in the morning. After breakfast cleared away an old frame and dug the corner for the Calceolarias. Lifted the syes, dug and replanted them and dug the rest of that corner. Fine day.

25th March
1874 Wed: Digging at the willow border. Some cuttings of Chrysanthemums sent away to Gordon Castle and to John Hardy. Bagra and Ingram and me took bone from the barns and sowed them on the onion ground at the Orchard and pointed it. After dinner we sowed some seeds in the Lower Garden; peas and carrots and spinach between the cabbage rows, two lines Broccoli, then beans, leeks and two lines of carrots where the celery was last year and a row of beans between them. A fine day.

26th March
1874 Thu: Preparing the onion field for sowing. Mackie up after breakfast and sowed them. Took off some grafts and took down with him apples of course while Ingram and me finished the field. Planting of potatoes commenced today beside the canal door. There was some put in the Vinery to sprout yesterday for the foot of the wall. Got a letter from Miss Cockburn and her CDV today.

Lime is used to reduce the acidity of soil; it helps some plants get the nutrients that they need; but it can also be used to kill off pests and fungi. As John and his colleagues were taking fruit in afterwards, the latter seems most likely.

It is thought Patterson and Gold refers to varieties of plums.

Soot can also be used as a means of preventing pests, but has the advantage it also acts as a fertiliser as it will yield salts of ammonia, potash and soda. Coal soot is specifically recommended for putting in an onion bed in several old gardening books, but it is also used at Duff House for many vegetables. *See also 31st March.*

We cannot trace the meaning of "syes".

For potatoes, John uses the word "sprout" for potatoes, often also called "chitting"; to try to force seed potatoes to start sending out shoots, before they are planted in the soil. He doesn't leave them very long, as the last of the potatoes were planted on 31st March.

We haven't been able to identify Miss Cockburn, neither in Banff before she might have moved away, and hence not elsewhere. The CDV shown is of an unknown young lady – called Nell - taken by a Banff photographer; this can't be Miss Cockburn as "6th May 1877" has been hand written on the back!
See also 31st Dec 1873.

27th March
1874 Fri: Fastening up all the rabbits holes around the fences in the morning. Planting potatoes after breakfast round to Mackie's garden but it came on rain and stopped us. Picking withered leaves in the Vinery in the afternoon.

28th March
1874 Sat: Finished the willow border in the morning with digging. Planting potatoes all day. A fine day.

29th March
1874 Sun: James Bagra came up in the forenoon and we went down and had a sail in the boat. At the Catholic Chapel in the evening. A fine day.

30th March
1874 Mon: Dug a piece in the morning. Potato planting in the forenoon; finished all but some between the young gooseberries. The rain stopped us. James Melvin away to a marriage. A hamper of Snow Drops sent away to Kintore. Very rough day.

31st March
1874 Tue: Commenced torching the Vinery. Last night had a fire on and syringed it, tied them up and pruned the roses etc about the door this morning. Planted the last of the potatoes after breakfast time. Down by watered the vines in the new vinery this forenoon. 7 caskfulls to the two Houses and 1 panful of liquid and three of hot to the cask which holds about 14 panfuls I suppose. Put on soot and pointed the piece before the little Vinery and sowed the Cabbage, Cauliflower, Sprouts, Greens etc. In the afternoon sowed a line of lettuces in the top at the foot of the dyke. Strong sunshine most of the day but rough.

Refer to the note on the page for 26th Oct 1874 for more information on the care of Vines, such as picking withered leaves and torching, based on information from the suppliers of the Vines to Duff House in 1873.

The Roman Catholic Chapel in 1873 was the same one as today on Sandyhills Road, it having been built in 1870. Thus when John went to a service 29th March 1874 it was still relatively new. The Minister was Rev Aeneas Chisholm.

The number of catholics in Banff at the time was believed to be about 200; the church was built with seating for 234.

Prior to 1870 there was a Catholic Chapel on Coldhome St, where No5 is today; at that time this was the edge of the town as the map extract shows. This had a limited capacity

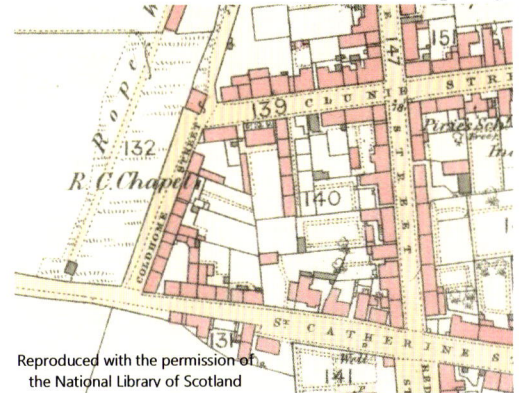

Reproduced with the permission of the National Library of Scotland

of just 50 people, so it is not surprising that they wanted a new and vastly improved building, which they achieved apparently for a cost at the time of £1300 – equivalent to only about £175,000 today when calculated with historic inflation rates.

James Melvin is a fellow gardener with John. His name appears several times before he departs on 5th Nov 1874. There is no Scottish record of him getting married himself in 1874, and he was back two days later, so presumably he was just attending a wedding.

1st April
1874 Wed: Raking off the prunings before the door. After breakfast taking off the dung off the asparagus then hoeing the young strawberries and raking the mud off them; hoed the rest of the old ones. Paid tonight, got £5, 8 s, the same as last. Paid the baker £2 2s. Gave Lewis Sellar 2s this day. Paid the milk. Melvine came home from the marriage. A fine day.

2nd April
1874 Thu: Fast day. Pyper, Smith, Wiseman, Mitchell and I went away up the length of the Corn Mill and some drank. Had Duncan the Keeper calling after came back from shooting too much. Fine day, very rough.

3rd April
1874 Fri: Shifting the Verbenas from the pots they were stuck in into boxes and Gasinias. Down in the afternoon helping riddle to dig his garden. Bagra and Ingram away to the Deer Park with Mackie's cow. Very rough day, some rain.

4th April
1874 Sat: Raking the weeds off the strawberries and hoeing and raking some spinach and turnips. Ingram away for Mackie's new cow. After dinner Bagra and me up at Raeburns for pots. Sowing annual seeds after we came back. A fine day.

John's pay was £5 8s per quarter. After six months he got a small increase. See also 8th Jan, 2nd Jul and 1st Oct 1874.

Lewis Sellar was the brother of Francis Sellar; they ran a drapers shop, sited on Low Street, in one of the shops as part of the Fife Arms Hotel, and lived at number 2 Bridge St (four brothers, an aunt and two servants.

Easter Sunday in 1874 was 5th April, generally the one day in the year when the Church of Scotland celebrated Holy Communion. Leading up to this there was a five day preparation period. The first of these was the Thursday before Easter – also Maundy Thursday – was known as "Fast Day", when the members of the congregation did little or no work – hence a holiday for John. The Friday was "Question Day" when there was a discussion about a verse of Scripture. Saturday was "Preparation Day" when communion tokens (see photo) were given out; the sacrament was celebrated on the Sunday, and a service of thanksgiving on the Monday brought the five day observance to an end. It seems in 1874 John took advantage of the day's holiday, but not the rest, not even going to church on Easter Sunday! *See also 22nd Oct 1874.*

Lord Fife's Corn Mill was on the River Deveron just south of the Rack. It is not identified on this map but at the end of the eighteenth century Earl Fife had made some adjustments to the lead off and back to the river, to help the fishermen that operated the Cruive Dyke.

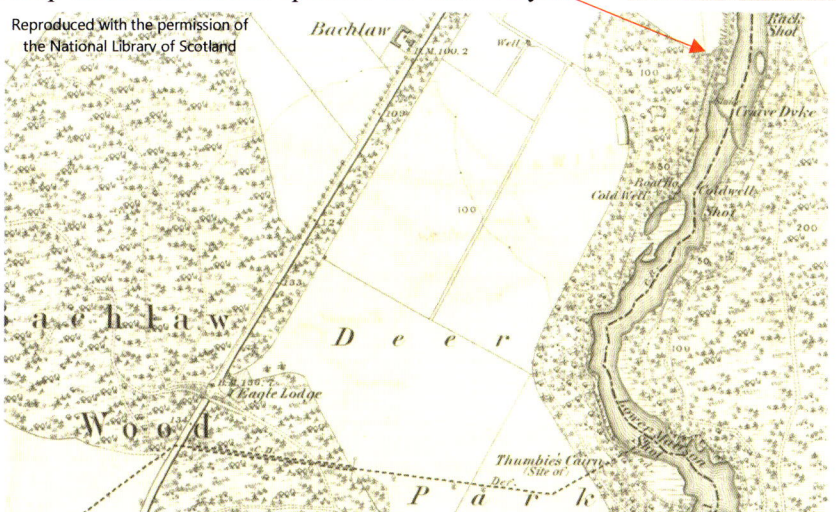

Reproduced with the permission of the National Library of Scotland

Deer Park – still called that – was southwest of The Rack (and the Corn Mill) up to what was Eagle Gate.

Raeburns – see note for 24th Nov 1873.

5th April
1874 Sun: Out the Sandyhill Road in the afternoon. Had a hunt with a squirrel in the Crow Wood. Not at Church today. Pretty dull day.

6th April
1874 Mon: Took down a hurleyful of the Old House in the Wood to Mackie's wife. Preparing the edges of the walk around the wall side for new boxwood. Laid some before night. A fine afternoon, rainy forenoon.

7th April
1874 Tue: Planting potatoes at the Orchard all day but did not finish them. At the Sishon today. Got the wea ane named Isabella I think it was. Fine day.

8th April
1874 Wed: Finished the potatoes today but some small pieces. Down about 1 o'clock preparing edges for boxwood the rest of the day. Fine day, some showers. Got coal yesterday.

9th April
1874 Thu: Planted the last of the potatoes this morning. Forking out crowfoot. Preparing edges for boxwood, Bagra and Ingram laying. Rough, cold morning but turned out a fine day; a good shower about night.

10th April
1874 Fri: Forking out crowfoot in the morning. After breakfast making edges in the forenoon. Finished them then laying in the afternoon. A fine day but a good shower in the afternoon.

11th April
1874 Sat: Forking out couch grass in the morning. Finished layout of the boxwood round the Walk at the wall side. Went away with Pyper tonight. A fine day.

Crow Wood are the woods south of Eagle Gate – see previous map. Eagle Gate as a house is still there, but in John's time there was also a bridge over the Foggie Road (A97).

"Old House in the Wood" could be that John took down a barrowful of wood that he had taken from an old house somewhere in the woods. We cannot identify any fruit or vegetable variety of that name.

John also visited this place on 3rd Mar, but we cannot identify it. The word may be Sishon or Lishon.

Isabella, John's wee one, had been born on 9th Feb, registered on 27th Feb, and maybe now baptised. John does seem very offhand about his offspring. *See also Chapter 2.*

Before buttercups gained that name, they used to be called crowfoot (which today applies more to some water loving plants of the Buttercup family), an invasive plant that spreads quickly in gardens using runners. (Picture from an 1849 original water colour)

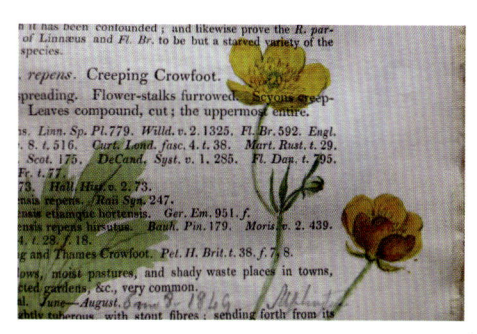

12th April
1874 Sun: At Netherbrae today. Home a little past 9 o'clock pm. Enjoyed myself fine. Got a fine day.

13th April
1874 Mon: Forking out weeds today in the morning. Sheeled up the Walk that we was laying the box on. Pointed a piece of ground for leeks and the bit that was made up for carrots. Sowed them. Bagra and Mackie was planting out the calceolarias and penstemons beside the Greenhouse. Limed the hotbed. A fine day, but dull, some cold.

14th April
1874 Tue: Forking out Bishop Weed before the Vinery after breakfast. Planted the potatoes we forced in the new Vinery at the foot of the wall. Two kinds, the other two was not grown enough. Sheeled up the broad edges of daisies on the Middle Walk, re-laying it new. A fine mild day. Some Mary Golds and helicrisum seeds put in tonight.

15th April
1874 Wed: Riddling the cinders in the stockhole and forking weeds before the Vinery. Preparing edges for daisies but came on rain and had to stop. Pulling out weeds in the Vinery till dinnertime. Put up a hotbed in the afternoon. Very mild but raining most of the day.

16th April
1874 Thu: Clipping the hedge before the Vinery in the morning. Finished the Hotbed after breakfast and went and finished the daisy edges. A very rough rainy day. Went home about 3 o'clock.

17th April
1874 Fri: Clipping hedges in the morning. After breakfast shifting geraniums Bijou into pots. Raked the daisies off the sides of the Walk and some other outs and ins. A very rough rainy day. Down at the Dreel Hall tonight big gun training

The Earl Fife owned a fishery at Netherbrae – near King Edward. John may have been visiting there or visiting a friend nearby.

Sheeled means shovelled.

Bishop Weed is often called ground elder. A very invasive plant, and very difficult to get rid of as even the tiniest bit of root will start growing again.

Mary Golds (written as two words) seems to be a wonderful example of John writing down a plant name as he hears it. The only time he refers to marigolds is previously on 12th Nov 1873 where "African Marygolds do very well for the centre".

Refer to the note for 17th March for Geranium Bijou.

Refer to the note for 27th Dec for the Dreel Hall = Drill Hall = Volunteer Hall.

John refers to Big Gun Training. The Banff Artillery Volunteers were equipped in 1874 with 24 pounder guns (see picture for a coastal defence gun – an old design). *See also the note for 25th July.*

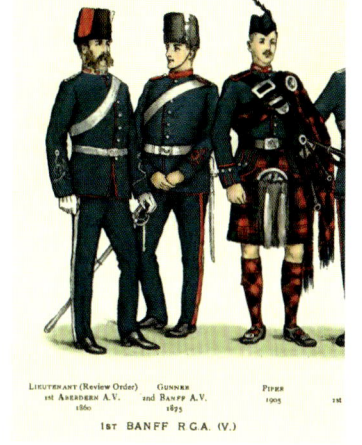

The uniforms – for the Banff Artillery Volunteers are shown in "The Records of the Scottish Volunteer Force" by Major-General Grierson.

18th April

1874 Sat: Clipping hedges in the morning. Watering the New Vineries today, 4 caskfulls in each and plant the rest of the forced potatoes at the wall side. Grafting the rest of the day. The ship went down today. A fine day. The onions that came from G McPherson planted tonight and three rows of cauliflower.

19th April

1874 Sun: Had Mitchell with us all night. Round by the Bridge of Alvah and the Crow Wood in the forenoon. Travelling about most of the day. At McDuff in the evening. A fine day, some slight showers in the forenoon.

20th April

1874 Mon: Grafting here in the morning, re-laying the bed chamomile. Took the flowering kind over to the corner at the Fruitroom, put them in beside some daisies and laid the place with daisies. Finished up the Walks in the afternoon. Commenced to dig the shrubbery border in the flower garden. A very mild day.

21st April

1874 Tue: Commenced to the shrubbery border, least we commenced it yesterday but was at it all day. Pruning some and raking leaves and digging. A fine day, strong sunshine all day.

22nd April

1874 Wed: Making the edges of the small flower garden before the door here ready for new boxwood. We dug the edges and took out the old box yesterday morning. Hoeing walks in the kitchen garden all day up at the back and grafted an apple tree to Goldsworth. Very warm day, strong sunshine.

The ship went down today is not a reference to sinking, but the launching of a ship, ie it went down the slip way. The ship was the schooner "*Baron Skene*", 83 foot long and 21 feet beam, single deck, two masted, wooden hull, classed with Lloyds Register of Shipping. This picture is of a sister ship, also built in Banff but two years later, called the "*Ban Righ*".

She was built by John and William Geddie, and as John writes in his diary was launched down the Banff harbour slip way. (NB Later on there was a shipyard at Greenbanks, but not in 1874). The photo below shows another schooner in Banff Harbour 12 years later, with the slip in the background.

Refer to the Note for 4th May as to what happened to the "*Baron Skene*".

We can find no G McPherson as a commercial nurseryman anywhere in Scotland at the time, so perhaps these came from Sir George Macpherson Grant of Ballindalloch.

See note for 5th April for Crow Wood.

Mr Goldsworth was the head gamekeeper, so presumably he wanted an apple tree in his garden.

23rd April
1874 Thu: Laying boxwood before the door here in the morning. Hoeing walks in the kitchen garden all forenoon. Raking in the afternoon. A fine day but not much sunshine.

24th April
1874 Fri: Laid the rest of the boxwood before the door. Took down a hurleyful of potatoes. Hoed the walk round the wall til the Vinery and among the frames. Grafted three seedling pear trees. Dug the phloxes in the afternoon, while the rest commencing hoeing the walks in the flower garden. Fine mild day, slight shower about dinnertime, no sun hardly.

25th April
1874 Sat: Giving the walks the finishing touch before the door here and preparing a field for grass seed. Melvine and me raking walks most of the day. The rest hoeing mostly in the flower garden. A fine day.

26th April
1874 Sun: Up at Mackie's in the forenoon. Took down his dahlias. Was at the church in the evening as I have not been for a good while back. Mr Bruce preaching text Malachi 3 v 8. A fine day, awful warm.

27th April
1874 Mon: Sowed a field of grass in the morning. Hoed and raked the last of the walks in the forenoon, all cleaned now but the canal one. Finished the shrubbery border, digging it. A fine day but no sunshine.

28th April
1874 Tue: In the morning sowed clover seed on the field that I sowed the grass in yesterday and dug up some weeds in another place. At the Rosery all day digging and cleaning it. A fine day, breezy.

Malachi Ch3 v8: "Will a man rob God? Yet ye have robbed me. But ye say, Wherein have we robbed thee? In tithes and offerings."

In the Banffshire Journal of this week (28th April 1874), they provide a list of all the significant landowners in Banffshire. Lord Fife is the second largest behind the Duke of Richmond and Gordon.

Name	Estimated Acreage of Property (Acres)	Gross Annual Value (£ s)
Sir Robert Abercromby, Forglen House	8053	6290 2
Rev. James Allan, Keith	7	49 10
Rev. Alexander Anderson, Marnoch	11	35 0
Trustees of Alex. Andrew, of Easterfield	108	105 0
Rev. William Asher, Inveraven	8	32 0
Banff Brewery Company, Banff	14	126 0
Burgh of Banff, Banff	46	255 8
Banff Cemetery Company, Banff	6	15 0
Banff Harbour Trustees, Banff (Harbour)	4	104 0
Kirk-Session of Banff, Banff	6	17 0
Banffshire Lunacy Board, Boyndie	20	260 0
James Barclay, of Buchromb, Mortlach, and 1, Cushion Court, Old Broad Street, London		
Trustees of late Wm. Bartlett, Banff	253	213 15
James Bisset, Macduff	2	82 10
Andrew Boyd, Castlebrae, St Fergus	2	6 13
Heritors of Boyndie Parish	2	21 8
Rev. William S. Bruce, Banff	1	1 0
F. W. Garden Campbell of Troup	9546	5712 9
Do. (Gardenstown Harbour)	1	82 0
Trustees of James Cassie, Banff	2	33 5
Trustees of late Alex. Chalmers, of Cluny	3069	2505 13
Rev. William Clapperton, Buckie	2	55 0
Alexander Clark, Macduff	1	10 0
Alex. Colville, 4, Low Street, Banff	2	70 5
George Cowie, Dufftown	2	80 0
Rev. James Cruden, Gamrie	17	35 0
Rev. J. A. Cruickshank, Mortlach	5	35 0
Parochial Board of Cullen	2	10 0
James Cumine, of Rattray	700	675 2
Major L. D. Gordon Duff, of Drummuir and Park	13053	7418 0
M. E. Grant Duff, of Eden, M.P.	7	20 6
Robert W. Duff, of Fetteresso, M.P.	2671	2346 19
Lieut.-Col. Geo. A. Ferguson, of Pitfour	10845	9446 12
Earl of Fife	72027	35879 13
Do. (Macduff Harbour)	5	500 0
Earl of Fife, and James Barclay, of Buchromb (Commonty)	400	(Included in values of Estates)
James Forbes, Portsoy	1	45 15
John Forbes, of Haddo	4773	3981 7
Trustees of Free Church of Forglen	1	10 0
John Forsyth, Old Keith	1	54 0
Rev. Hugh Fraser, Alvah	10	40 0
Mrs Fraser, of Thorax, F.C. Manse, Kirkwall	171	164 10
Heritors of Gamrie Parish	2	2 0
Trustees of Rev. George Garioch	275	148 0
James Geddes, Portsoy	1	23 10
Rev. Jas. Glennie, Chapelton, Inveraven	7	10 0
Trustees of Church of Glenrinnes	3	15 0
Adam Hay Gordon, of Avochie	2171	1528 15
Heirs of Rev. Alex. Gordon, Forglen	10	35 0
John Gordon, of Cluny	2734	2724 9
John Gordon, of Cairnfield	3175	1362 12
John Gordon, Macduff	2	215 0
Sir Robt. G. Gordon, of Letterfourie, Bart.	1715	1937 3
Do. (Buckie Harbour)	5	25 0
Sir George Macpherson Grant, of Ballindalloch, Bart.	14225	3616 16
Rev. James Grant, Kirkmichael	14	30 0
Rev. James Grant, Fordyce	10	46 0
Hon. Lewis A. Grant, of Grant	31	1285 0
William Grant, of Wester Elchies	4212	1325 15
Trustees of Wm. Grant, of Beldorney	3449	1098 18
Miss Macpherson Grant, of Aberlour	855	722 15
Great North of Scotland Railway Company	321	10696 0
Wm. Green, Lynburn, Aberlour	1	26 0
John Harvey, of Carnousie	3424	3296 13
George P. Hay, of Edintore	350	150 0
Rev. George Henderson, Cullen	7	43 0
Highland Railway Company	22	605 0
Rev. Wm. Hunter, Macduff	2	34 0
Sir James M. Innes, of Edingight, Bart.	3160	1882 16
Lieut. Robt. Innes, Charlestown, Aberlour	1	12 0
Thomas G. K. Innes, of Netherdale	3771	2690 6
Heritors of Inveraven Parish	2	10 0
The Sueckeners of Invermarkie	2	2 6
John Johnston, Brockholes House, Salop	2	24 0
Heritors and Par. Board of Keith Parish	2	2 0
Mrs Marjory A. Grant Kinloch, of Arndilly	5895	2864 19
Trustees of Al. Kynoch of Greentown	221	103 6
Geo. & Geo. Kynoch, Keith	15	256 0
Geo. Kynoch, jun., Keith	3	16 0
John Laing, Charlestown, Aberlour	7	64 10
Trustees of Lawtie's Mortification, Cullen	9	51 1
Rev. James Ledingham, Boyndie	11	32 0
Geo. A. Young Leslie of Kininvie	1941	996 12
Capt. Hans G. Leslie of Dunlugas	1568	1477 6
Andrew Longmore of Linksfield	51	83 0
William Longmore, Keith	4	112 10
Trustees of Lorimer's Mortification, Cullen	1	10 0
Donald M'Culloch, Asylum, Banff	5	40 14
Peter M'Donald, Charlestown, Aberlour	1	65 19
Macduff Commercial Company	2	193 7
Magistrates and Town Council of Macduff	2	4 0
Rev. James M'Intosh, Deskford	7	25 0
Rev. James M'Lachlan, Rathven	13	40 0
Rev. John M'Lennan, Tomintoul	2	13 0
Rev. James M'Voar, Ordiquhill	3	20 0
William Marshall, Buckie	5	35 5
Rev. Alex. Mason, Boharm	5	6 12
Rev. Wm. Mason, Botriphnie	8	23 0
Rev. John Mitchell, St Fergus	11	34 0
Rev. Robt. Mohr, Rothiemay	2	83 0
Morayshire Railway Company	4154	3002 4
Alexander Morison of Bognie	582	321 15
James Morrison of Culvie		
Joseph J. L. L. Morrison, and Maria C. S. Morrison of Tolie	398	310 12
Heritors of Mortlach Parish	1	2 0
Alexander Murdoch, Banff	16	18 0
James Muterer, Old Manse, Boharm	1	11 10
James Nicol, Turriff	2	2 0
Trustees of Church of Ord	2088	1888 13
John Ramsay of Straloch	260	265 0
Henry Alex. Rannie of Greenlaw	1	5 0
Heritors of Rathven Parish	5	46 0
Daniel Reid, Hazlewood, Blackhillock	1	10 0
Duke of Richmond	139,950	29,831 18
Do. do., Portgordon Harbour	2	50 0
Heirs of William Ross, Cullen	1	24 0
Rev. John Russell, Grange	1	15 0
Trustees of St Fergus Free Church	48,939	33,878 6
Earl of Seafield	290	16
Do. do. (Harbours)	7	390 0
Rev. James Sellar, Aberlour	6	35 0
Robert S. Kynoch Shand, Keith	5	11 0
Ann Shand, Wellfield, Banff	5	20 0
Rev. Robert Shanks, F.C. Manse, Buckie	2	135 10
James Simpson, Banff	11	171 5
Robert Simpson of Cobairdy	631	495 0
William Smith, Schoolhouse, Gartly	1	16 0
George Smollet, Hilton of Blacklaw, Banff	4	11 0
Heirs of James Souter, Banff	1	165 5
Rev. John Souter, Inverkeithney	14	55 0
Rev. G. Stephen, Schoolhouse, Fordyce	17	25 0
Andrew Steuart of Auchlunkart	6329	4449 13
Alexander Stewart of Laithers	3	10 0
Capt. James Stewart of Lesmurdie	2075	460 9
William James Tayler of Glenbarry	313	264 0
James Taylor of Greenskairs	406	388 0
John F. S. Taylor, London	3	78 10
Rev. James Thomson, Gartly	15	47 0
Mrs Pollard Urquhart of Craigston	16	22 10
Alexander Walker, Banff	3	167 5
Peter Walker, Dufftown, Mortlach	1	43 5
Alexander Watt, Macduff	8	69 10
Trustees of Charles Watt, Crombie	627	624 12
James Watt of Whitehill	474	290 14
Alexander Wilson, Inchgower, Rathven	7	158 0
Rev. A. F. Wilson, Banff	20	137 4
Trustees of James Wilson, Banff	4	42 4

Page 133

29th April
1874 Wed: Not much doing in the morning. At the Rosery all day us three finished it in the afternoon. the foreman was not up. First night of drill in the Park. Very warm day.

30th April
1874 Thu: Awful tired this morning; at the Longmore's last. Did not rise til breakfast time. Raking the potato border by the canal door before the potatoes come through the ground. Hoeing strawberries afternoon. Mackie was sowing turnips. A fine day but colder some today.

1st May
1874 Fri: Finishing the hoeing of the strawberries. Hoeing of spinach and raspberries in the afternoon. A fine day. Got a pair of new Sunday boots, lacing one tonight.

2nd May
1874 Sat: Dunged and dug the piece around the standard cherry tree. Dug the herbs.

3rd May
1874 Sun: Ingram away from home today. Rose about 11 o'clock. Over at Macduff in the afternoon seeing the new ship that was smashed on the rocks this morning. Not at church today. Dull cold day.

4th May
1874 Mon: Not doing much in the morning. Pinting the flower border in the forenoon. Hoeing the walk by the canal door in the afternoon. A pretty cold day. No sunshine.

The word "Park" is generally used to describe Duff House Park. There was a lot of open flat land around Duff House on which soldiers could march and drag equipment. The Earl of Fife was the Honorary Colonel of the 1st Banff Royal Garrison Artillery Volunteers. *See notes for 27th Dec & 17th April.*

The Longmores were corn and seed merchants in Banff, as well as farmers and cattle dealers, and ran a General Merchant store on George St in Banff. Also House Furnishers with a shop on High St.

The new ship that John refers to was the same one he had already mentioned on 18th April – the schooner "*Baron Skene*". Baron Skene was a title given to James the 5th Earl Fife in 1857. It enabled him to sit in the House of Lords, as the Earl Fife title is in the Irish peerage. While 5th Earl Fife didn't have too rocky a life, the ship bearing his name was not so fortunate.

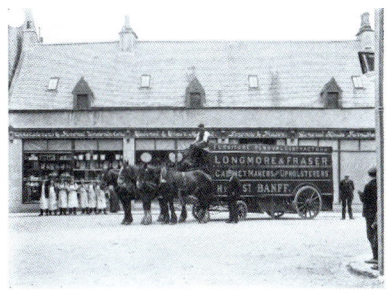

On 3rd May 1874 she sailed from Banff in ballast, bound for St Petersburg. Under the command of Captain W Mason she managed to sail about a mile and is believed to have hit rocks to the southwest of Collie Rocks. Not a particularly auspicious start for a brand new vessel.

The reason for her hitting the rocks is not known; John Donaldson describes the weather every day and just records it as "dull cold day"; if it had been windy he would have used the word "rough".

She was assisted off the rocks and into Macduff harbour. She was repaired – the Lloyds Register report is on record - and must have done some voyages, but her luck really didn't improve. On 3rd January 1875, carrying a cargo of coal from Newcastle to Banff, she capsized 4 miles east of Kinnaird Head during a severe gale. All hands were lost, including Captain Mason.

A few years later, a Miss M'Donald gave a recitation of the "Loss of Baron Skene" at a soiree in the Seafield Church in Portknockie (according to the Aberdeen Journal in 1891). We have not been able to track down a copy of this poem, or song, or story!

Pinting is generally pointing, presumably meaning similar to hoeing.

5th May

1874 Tue: Forking out weeds in the morning. Finished the canal walk, hoeing and raking it after which we went to the flower garden. Sowed mignonette around the edges of the dahlia border. Pretty cold weather being the gab of May.

6th May

1874 Wed: Pinting over the ground and sowing peas and carrots in the morning. After breakfast prepared the beds in the border of the flower garden. Took off the oldest frame and prepared it for cucumbers. Repaired the floor of the potato shed. Very unsteady day, sometimes sunshine and the next time raining. Very cold.

7th May

1874 Thu: Commenced to dig before the door here. Cut the half of the plot of grass and trenched it. Sowed carrots and beet in it. After dinnertime I was at the smithy with Ingram's scythe, got a new blade and got it hung. Commenced to hoe the shrubbery border. Cold wrecky days always.

9th May

1874 Fri: Commenced cutting the flower garden this morning. Cutting edges and raking off the grass the rest of the day. Cold always but a fine day.

9th May

1874 Sat: Watering the vines today and pinting the beds in the horse shoe. Planted the last of the potatoes, a few that was always forgotten and staked some peas. Bagra and Ingram went away to Troup tonight. Always cold, no sunshine today.

Mignonettes One of the drawbacks of geraniums, and to some extent dahlias, is that in hot weather they give off an odour, particularly if touched by the voluminous skirts of ladies. Hence some plants near paths were often intermingled with mignonette, as their small green scented flower spikes were not visually very noticeable (thanks to the garden historian Sue Gregory for highlighting this practice).

The gab of May is a Scots language phrase for a spell of bad weather about the beginning of May. The same sort of meaning is obviously meant two days later when John refers to "wrecky" weather – a term perhaps referring to that fact that it can wreck ships.

The 1867 and 1877 Directories for Banff list five blacksmith's in Banff, so John could have meant any one of these:

    William Blyth – Reid St
    John Dawson – Bridge St
    John Fraser – Bridge St
    Laing Gray – Low Shore
    William Reid – Old Market Place

as well as Banff Foundry. The 1867 Ordnance Survey map of Banff clearly labels the Old Smiddy in Old Market Place as "Smithy"; there is another just off North Castle St onto Carmelite St. Previously the Old Smiddy, now the Silversmiths, used to be a meal-house, ie for storing grain.

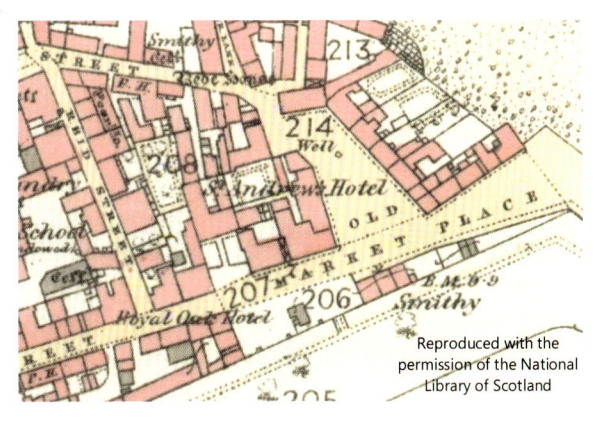

Reproduced with the permission of the National Library of Scotland

John refers to the Smithy again on 17th August when he went again with his scythe.

Note: some writers refer to the Old Smiddy as only becoming a Smithy in 1902 but the 1867 map suggests the 1902 date is in error.

For Troup refer to the note for 11th Oct 1874.

10th May
1874 Sun: Mitchell was up with me last night, stopped til dinnertime. Not at church today. A fine day, very warm, strong sunshine. Mackie was up thinning out some of the shoots of the vines last Friday, I forgot to mention it.

11th May
1874 Mon: Down in the morning cutting grass. Finished edges the rest of the day. Cold day, slight showers.

12th May
1874 Tue: Down at the rosery levelling the mole heaps in the morning. Getting off cuttings off the edges and pinting beds. Cold day.

13th May
1874 Wed: Down in the morning cutting grass, raking and cutting edges the rest of the day and pinting beds. A very dull day. Cold always.

14th May
1874 Thu: Digging before the door in the morning. Raking beds in the forenoon in the flower garden and hoeing the shrubbery till dinnertime. Raining in the afternoon. I came home at dinnertime. The rest commenced to take out Dante Lions out among the grass but stopped and went to the House's. More mild today.

15th May
1874 Fri: Forking Dante Lions out among the grass in the flower garden. Got the large roller over from the farm and rolled the grass. Fine day.

16th May
1874 Sat: Down in the morning cutting grass. Finished the cutting today. Raked it off and cut the edges. The foreman was not with us in the afternoon. The Gladiolies have been planted out today or yesterday. A fine day. Was up winding up the old church clock tonight.

Dante Lions is another of John's own quite fun spellings, obviously meaning dandelions. We could find no old reference to them being called "Dante Lions". They do have medicinal properties, and the flowers can be used for a yellow dye; hence they were originally deliberately planted, although generally today, and for gardeners in John's time, they were a nuisance. The four times John mentions them he always uses the same spelling.

St Mary's, Banff Parish Church, was originally built in 1790, although the tower and spire weren't finished until the 1840s. The previous church, St Mary's, was just off Carmelite St – where the "Banff Aisle" still stands in the graveyard.

The clock had been removed from the old St Mary's before the present church was built. It may be this old church clock that John refers to.

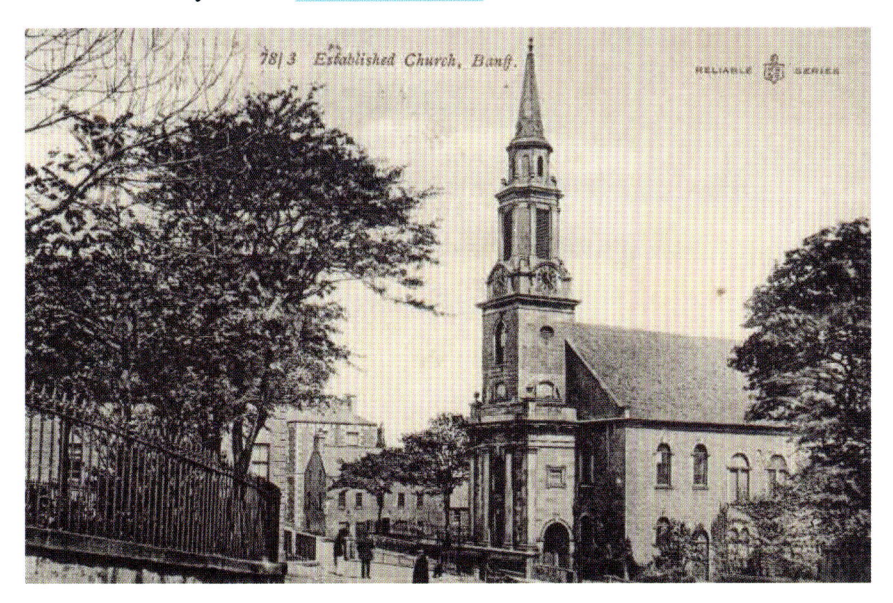

17th May
1874 Sun: Rose today about 10 o'clock a.m. Didn't got to church today. Away looking for wild flowers in the forenoon; no other thing worth speaking about. A very warm day.

18th May
1874 Mon: Pinted over the last of the beds in the flower garden. Took out the Dante Lions and rolled it. Was down playing at the beat and throwing the hammer this evening. A fine day.

19th May
1874 Tue: Taking out Dante Lions out of the walks in the Orchard in the morning. Finished the rolling of the flower garden. Rolled the braes with the little stone roller. Finished hoeing the shrubbery. A fine day.

20th May
1874 Wed: Raking the shrubbery border and burying the rakings in the forenoon. Bagra and Ingram down at Mr Mackie's at not a very fancy job. Melvin and me raking. A fine day.

21st May
1874 Thu: Burying the rakings of the shrubbery border what we did not finish yesterday. Bagra and Ingram weeding onions the rest of the day in the north border. Melvin and me drawing lines around the horseshoe for bedding and hoeing among the earliest sown peas. A fine day.

22nd May
1874 Fri: Preparing the piece before the Vinery for French beans in the morning. Hoeing strawberries in the forenoon and gooseberries and raked least tossed there. At the market in the afternoon. Got some drunk toward evening. Fine day.

23rd May
1874 Sat: Rose about half 10 o'clock. Dug the corner beside the tank. Put up a hotbed. Made a bed for celery to be pricked out in, some pricked out. Pretty dull day. Some humdrum in spirit today.

Drawing lines in the Horseshoe, the distinctly shaped bed in the lower Airlie Gardens, refers to the method of ribbon planting, ie lines of different flowers.

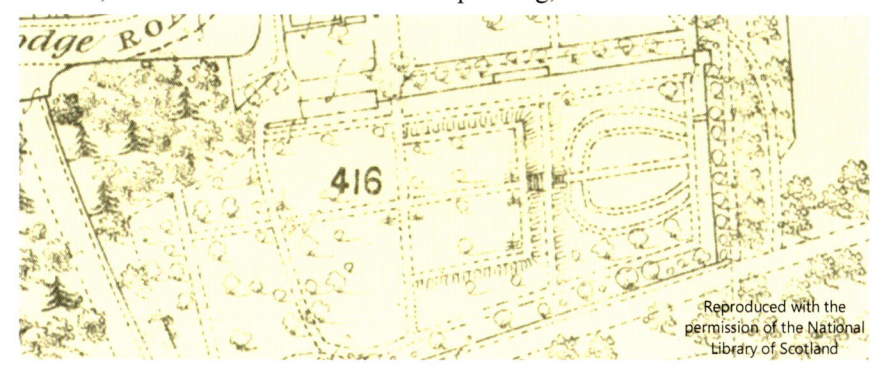

Reproduced with the permission of the National Library of Scotland

We know the planting plan for 1873 because John took the plants out (see the Note for 12th Nov 1873), and also for 1874, the ones he is about to plant this May (planned in November 1873, planted 27th May 1874).

1873 (only 5 ribbons):
Outside: Cerastium
            Verbenas ("they didn't do very well at all")
            Blue Salvia ("did very well")
            Trentham Rose Geranium ("did well")
Centre: Antirrhinum ("they did not do well; a lot of them did not come")

1874 (6 ribbons, also box hedge laid 5th to 8th Mar):
Outside: Alyssum
            Dwarf Nasturtium
            Calceolarias
            Jonquilla
            Scarlet Penstemons
Centre: African Marigolds

Refer to Index B for a full list of all the flowers mentioned in the Diary.

24th May

1874 Sun: Rose about 11 o'clock. Went down after breakfast to the other bothie to see what was said about stopping the chimney and lifting the starlings to the top of the tree which Ingram and me did last night. Stopped at home all day til the evening. Was not at church today. Pretty cold rough day.

25th May

1874 Mon: Pretty long in rising this morning again. Did nothing before breakfast. After commenced at Mackie's and hoed potatoes all day. Cold rough day.

26th May

1874 Tue: Term day. Cleaned out Cleland's dung hill in the forenoon. Hoed potatoes the rest of the day. Fine day.

27th May

1874 Wed: Hoed potatoes in the forenoon. Commenced the bedding out in the afternoon for the first time. Put out 6 lines around the Shoe. A fine day but always dry, no rain.

28th May

1874 Thu: Down in the morning bedding. Finished the Shoe in the morning and the border on the other side of the door from the dahlias filled the narrow border. At the sides of the middle walk from top to bottom of the garden. In the evening we planted the two lower ovals that completed the day's work. Fine day.

29th May

1874 Fri: Planted the rest of the ovals and all the little circles through the day. In the evening planted the borders down from the Vinery to the end. Fine day.

Starlings can cause complete blockage of a chimney, and as it was necessary to keep the Vinery heated – 24th May John called a cold day – it would have had to be cleared to ensure the vines were kept at the right temperature.

Since 1886 the Scottish Term days – quarter days – are 28th Feb, 28th May, 28th Aug and 28 Nov. Traditionally these were days that leases would begin or end, servants hired or dismissed, and interest on loans came due. 26th May is a legacy Term Day based on Whitsun in the Julian Calendar, until the Gregorian Calendar was adopted in Scotland in 1599.

This may or may not be any sort of realistic imitation of what it may have looked like, when John and his colleagues finished the Shoe, based on the planting plan from November and given in the Note against 21st May 1874.

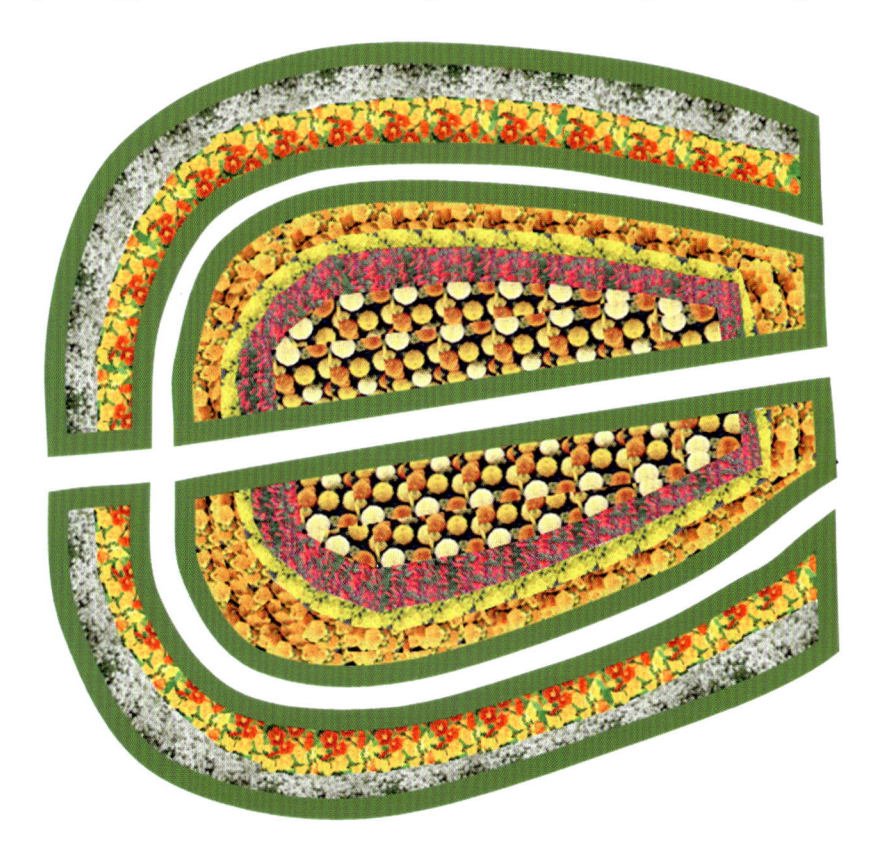

30th May

1874 Sat: Forgot to mention that I sowed the French beans yesterday morning. Sent down the blankets this morning to get them washed. Planting out some flowers in our own garden here. This morning after breakfast put in the stakes for the dahlias. Planted some small pieces about the Vinery. Planted the geranium beds next the Vinery in the border and in the afternoon planted the dahlias; there was a dozen came from Park today. Fine day.

31st May

1874 Sun: Nothing of any importance today. At the Church in the evening. A fine day.

1st June

1874 Mon: Hoeing gooseberries today and several other pieces, raspberries etc. Fine day.

2nd June

1874 Tue: The first day at the Orchard hoeing potatoes all day. Weeding onions in the morning. They were tossing weeds and hoeing in the other garden. A fine day but very dry, fine for weeds.

3rd June

1874 Wed: Hoeing today again. Got all the low garden hoed here. Weeding in the morning the onions. They were hoeing in the other garden pieces for cabbages etc.

4th June

1874 Thu: Up in the morning between 4 and 5 o'clock and down to the rosery cutting it. Through with it by dinnertime. Came home and hoed. Down bathing in Deveron twice today; for the first time trying to swim. Warm today.

Gooseberries. John had named several varieties on 4th March (see note). Many of these are not varieties that are still available, but those with photos below can still be found in specialist nurseries. John mentions 11 varities but there were hundreds.

Antagonist. White. Won heaviest berry at some Gooseberry Shows.

Careless. White. One of the most handsome gooseberries, and probably the most reliable cropper, it bears heavy crops of very large, smooth-skinned creamy white fruit that have a superb flavour. It is early to fruit, but does not perform at its best in shade.

Conquering Hero. Red. Often came second to London in Gooseberry Shows..

Dan's Mistake. Red. Mid-season. Red, very large oval, hairy fruit with excellent flavour. Spreading habit. Mostly fruits on the last season's wood.

Drill. Yellow.

Leveller. Yellow. One of the best yellows, the smooth and well-flavoured fruits are borne freely on this the most favourite of mid-season varieties. A must if you are growing gooseberries for the first time, as it combines excellent quality with great fertility.

London. Red. This variety produces a good heavy red berry which is round and smooth. Fairly dwarf growth - responds well to feeding and mulching.

Ludimar Worcester "were thumpers" according to John.

Shiner. No information found.

Stockwell. Green.

Telegraph. Green. Large, elongated dark green fruit.

5th June
1874 Fri: Hoeing all day among potatoes here at the Orchard. They were hoeing down in the other garden and they planted the gourds in front of the Vinery. A fine day, would be a deal better of a shower.

6th June
1874 Sat: Hoeing all day again up here. Thinned the first of the grapes but they were hardly out of flower. They were hoeing down in the other in the other garden and preparing ground for cabbage. Down at dinnertime bathing. A fine day.

7th June
1874 Sun: Up in the morning and at the sea for the first time bathing but some cold. Bathed in Deveron again about the middle of the day. Was not church today. Fine day. A slight shower about dinnertime.

8th June
1874 Mon: Hoeing potatoes all day at the Orchard. Old Kippin was up today hoeing walks down in the other garden. Down in the evening at the Boat House bathing. A fine day but no rain.

9th June
1874 Tue: Hoeing all day, least in the forenoon. Raining in the afternoon. Thinning some of the grapes in the Vinery. Hoeing walks down in the other garden in the forenoon; great in need of the rain.

10th June
1874 Wed: Down in the morning at the other garden planting cabbage and down through the day earthing up potatoes. Fine day.

11th June
1874 Thu: Raining in the morning. Commenced sheeling at the back of the Vinery. Down through the day working at the canal walk. Came home after dinner. Thinned some grapes in the evening. Very cold.

The Boat House was on the river a few hundred yards from Banff Bridge.
Refer to the photo in Chapter 4.
There was another boat house near to The Rack.

This old photo shows a family at leisure on the River Deveron, the child looking like he is going bathing.

Sheeling = shovelling.

Gaveney Brae (before the Distillery was built)

12th June
1874 Fri: Down at the other garden today. Again at the canal walk all day. Finished it. A fine day, not very warm.

13th June
1874 Sat: Down at the other garden again today. Earthing up potatoes all day. Finished the border and two or three of the breaks. Took out the straw out of the back elevating holes of the new Vineries. A fine day.

14th June
1874 Sun: Up in the morning and down at the sea but did not bathe today in the morning. Bathed in Deveron in the forenoon. At the church in the evening Mr B preaching text in Luke Ch 18 v 9 etc. I think my uncle was down today in the afternoon. I was up at W.C's mother's in the evening. Fine day.

15th June
1874 Mon: At the Orchard today all day. Hoeing some potatoes and earthing up, down at the other garden. A fine day.

16th June
1874 Tue: Hoeing the borders round the walks in the low garden. At the Orchard hoeing and raking among walks down in the other garden. A fine day.

17th June
1874 Wed: Commenced to hoe the walks at the Orchard today. Hoeing all day. Hoeing down in the other garden. A fine day.

Mr B is presumably Rev Bruce, the Minister of Banff. Two books have been published by, or about, Rev Bruce:

"Bruce of Banff" was published in 1934, written by Adam Fergusson.

"Reminiscences of Seventy Years" was published in 1929, and is Rev Bruce relating his own thoughts about his whole career.

There are some paintings of Rev Bruce. His photo and signature are given in the front of his book.

See also the note for 30th Oct 1873.

Luke Ch18 vs9 to 14: "And he spake this parable unto certain which trusted in themselves that they were righteous, and despised others:
Two men went up into the temple to pray; the one a Pharisee, and the other a publican.
The Pharisee stood and prayed thus with himself, God, I thank thee, that I am not as other men are, extortioners, unjust, adulterers, or even as this publican. I fast twice in the week, I give tithes of all that I possess.
And the publican, standing afar off, would not lift up so much as his eyes unto heaven, but smote upon his breast, saying, God be merciful to me a sinner.
I tell you, this man went down to his house justified rather than the other: for every one that exalteth himself shall be abased; and he that humbleth himself shall be exalted."

W.C. would be William Craig. John has spent two other times visiting William's mother, but we have been unable to identify him (see note for 29th Jun 1874).

18th June
1874 Thu: Hoeing walks all day and raking. Got a newspaper from Australia last night and a letter from James McBean tonight. Hoeing down at the other place. Fine day.

19th June
1874 Fri: Finished the walks in the low garden. Up here this morning and then before the door. Hoed the onions today and started the broad walk at the back of ... (text missing) Fine day.

20th June
1874 Sat: Started to cut the edges of the broad walk at the Orchard this morning. Cut the edges with the edging box. Raked them up and raked the bit that was hoed before at the back of the Vinery. Ingram and Bagra away to Troup today. A fine day.

21st June
1874 Sun: Down at the lower bothy all night, served in the kitchen today. At the church in the evening; the text in Luke, I forget where. Took five moles today. A good shower today.

22nd June
1874 Mon: Down at the other garden today laying strawberries and staking peas. The girls from the House was over today. A fine day.

23rd June
1874 Tue: Sheeled the Broad Walk up at the Orchard here today and shifting plants down at the other place. Bought my new watch last night and went down for her tonight. Fine day.

24th June
1874 Wed: Up in the morning and down cutting grass in the flower garden. Cleared it up in the forenoon and shifted plants in the afternoon. Banff v Keith Cricket Club in the park today. Banff gained.

Getting a newspaper from Australia was obviously noteworthy for John, but we don't know the relevance; presumably a relative or friend having emigrated there. *See also 2nd and 3rd Dec 1873.*

James McBean was a previous apprentice gardener at Duff House, two years older than John. We don't know where he had moved on to.

> Late 19th century view from Doune Hill down the Deveron valley showing Duff House
>
> DEVERON VALLEY AND DUFF HOUSE, BANFF.

Sheeled means shovelled; the Broad Walk at the Orchard was chuckies (gravel) of some sort. On 25th June John rakes the Broad Walk, and on 8th Aug he "tosses" it..

There was just one jeweller in Banff at the time, Simpsons on Bridge St, hence where John presumably purchased his watch. Refer to 2nd July as John only paid for this watch after he was paid at the start of July.

Although Banff won against the Keith Cricket Club, it was not reported in the Banffshire Journal the following week!

25th June
1874 Thu: Down cutting grass today again. Up and bathe before breakfast. Cleaned up the grass. Hoed walks in the afternoon. I came home at dinnertime. Planted vegetable marrows. Raked the Broad Walk.

26th June
1874 Fri: Up at the Orchard today all day. Hoeing some of the narrow walks in the upper garden. Hoeing walks down in the flower garden today. A fine day, greatly in want of a shower.

27th June
1874 Sat: Up about 5 o'clock in the morning cutting grass. Finished the cutting today. Cleared up the grass in the forenoon. Earthed up some potatoes that was left and came home. Ingram earthed up the peach border. The new Vinery border was cleared today. Fine day.

28th June
1874 Sun: Up in the morning and down at the sea bathing and in Deveron in the forenoon. Not at church today. The girls from the House was up in the afternoon. A fine warm day.

29th June
1874 Mon: Up early in the morning cutting grass. Finished it today. Down at the sea bathing in the morning. Cleaned it up and came home at dinnertime. Thinned grapes the most of the afternoon went over to Mr Craig's mother's in the evening with the books. Fine day.

30th June
1874 Tue: Earthed up a few potatoes in the morning. Down at the rosery all forenoon. Myself hoed the beds. Thinning the grapes in the afternoon "as they were pretty much in need". A fine day.

1st July
1874 Wed: Down at the other gardens today netting the strawberries. A fine day.

A riverside woodland path in the Duff House woods

Mr Craig's mother refers to William Craig who unfortunately we have not been able to trace. Other times he has visited William Craig's mother (29th Nov, 7th Dec, 14th Jun) John has referred to him as William; the use of "Mr" on this occasion suggests William was older, perhaps a more senior gardener, to John.
However a Margaret Craig, widow, age 68 in 1874, lived with her daughter aged 44, at 36 Boyndie Street, both of them working as Dressmakers.
But we have not been able to track Margaret's husband; she lived there, alone except for her spinster daughter, since at least 1841.
No other female Craig's are recorded in Banff at the time.

2nd July
1874 Thu: Down at the other gardens today digging the celery ridges and dunging them in the forenoon. Staking phloxes and gladioli's in the afternoon. A fine day. Got our pay today; I got £5 13s. Paid my watch.

3rd July
1874 Fri: At the Orchard today hoeing the currant border in the upper half, weeding onions, thinning grapes etc. A fine day.

4th July
1874 Sat: Up today by 4 o'clock thinning grapes. Finished them today. Mr Mackie was up this morning but he did not stop minutes. I thinned out leaves off the lateral shoots to let in more air to the House. Hoeing some of the currant brakes in the lower garden at the Orchard.

5th July
1874 Sun: Up in the morning and down at the sea bathing and in the Deveron in the forenoon. At the church in the evening. A fine day.

6th July
1874 Mon: Up at the Orchard today, hoeing and weeding onions. Lord Fife's birthday. Down at the supper in the evening. A fine day.

7th July
1874 Tue: At the Orchard today; finished weeding onions. Hoeing in the low gardens here. A fine day.

£5 13s is a slight rise from his previous pay of £5 8s per quarter (see 8th Jan and note for it; also 1st April and 1st October.

John had collected his watch on 23rd June (see note); unfortunately he doesn't say how much he paid for it.

Lord Fife, James Duff, 5th Earl Fife, 5th Baron Braco of Kilbryde, was born on 6th July 1814, so this was his 60th birthday.

The supper that John attended was quite a grand and formal occasion, reported by the Banffshire Journal as follows:

> "The out-door employees of the Right Hon. the Earl of Fife were entertained last night to supper on the occasion of the anniversary of the birth of his lordship. The supper took place at the Barnyards, Duff House, and there were about 90 present. Mr Goldsworth occupied the chair, and after having given the usual loyal and patriotic toasts, proposed the toast of the evening, the health of the Right Honourable the Earl of Fife. The toast was drunk to with enthusiasm. The Chairman also proposed the health of the Right Honourable the Viscount Macduff, MP, which was cordially received. Among the other toasts given were the health of the Hon. George Skene Duff, and of the commissioners and factors on the estate. The entertainment was provided by Mr Hutchinson of the Market Inn, Banff, and was of a most sumptuous character. A very pleasant evening was spent by the company."

This photograph is James, 5th Earl Fife, in 1863. Courtesy of National Galleries of Scotland.

8th July
1874 Wed: At the Orchard today hoeing the potatoes again; them that is not earthed up.

9th July
1874 Thu: At the Orchard today hoeing and raking the piece before the door etc. A fine day.

10th July
1874 Fri: Hoeing round the edges of the walks beneath the gooseberries at the Orchard etc. Shooting blackbirds etc. A fine day. Very dry.

11th July
1874 Sat: Planted some cabbage at the Orchard where I sowed the carrots. Shooting blackies. Mr Hardie came with the last train tonight. Went over a bit with him. Very dry, some hot.

12th July
1874 Sun: Heavy rain in the morning. Went down to the sea and bathed after went over. At the church in the evening. "A fine day after the shower".

13th July
1874 Mon: Earthed up some potatoes in the morning. Down today at the other garden pulling strawberries for Duff House in the forenoon. Thinning out the shoots of the Rasps and tying them up. Mr Hardy was here today. A fine day.

Mr Hardie had left Banff on 11th Nov 1873 when John had gone with him to Banff Station. He may have been a previous gardener that John had worked with early on at Duff House.

Banff (Harbour) Station was where it says it was, below the Banff Battery. The station, and the adjacent gasometer, are no longer there, but the route of the track west along Banff Links can easily be followed, and walked. Trains ran from 1859 to 1968.

Banff Bridge Station, with trains south towards Aberdeen from 1860, was the end terminus of the line before 1872, when the line was extended into Macduff.

Macduff Station, built 1872; closed 1st Oct 1951.

14th July

1874 Tue: Down at the other garden today. Tied up the last of the rasps and pulled some strawberries. A fine day.

15th July

1874 Wed: At the Orchard today hoeing sundry places all through the garden today. A fine day.

16th July

1874 Thu: Commenced to pull blackberries at the Orchard this morning. Pulled 3 boxes and took them down before dinnertime. Pulling currants round the wall in the afternoon. Fine day.

17th July

1874 Fri: Down at the other garden today. Tied up and pinched the shoots of the apricots in the forenoon. Did the same to the pear and cherry trees round the vegetable hillock. Came home at 5 o'clock and shut my Vinery. Fine day.

18th July

1874 Sat: Earthed up potatoes at the Orchard in the morning. Went away with the train to Elgin, Monday being Banff holiday. Fine day, very hot.

19th July

1874 Sun: Competition at Banff today among the Volunteers. At Lesmurdie today, stopped there till 2 o'clock, then came till Fochabers with the mail train and went to Gordon Castle. Awful warm.

Based on a report in the Banffshire Journal, one of the main activities of the people of Banff and Macduff at this local summer holiday was to catch the train and visit somewhere else – all business in the towns is reported as being suspended.
The Banffie focusses on how many people left the town compared to the holiday in 1873. *See the previous page for notes on the stations.*

From Banff Bridge Station:
Saturday, 212 excursion tickets were issued, only about two thirds of the previous year;
Monday, 274 excursion tickets, with 98 passengers on the first train of the day. This was apparently about the same number as 1873, but this year they went on shorter journeys.

From Macduff Station (last stop after Banff Bridge):
Saturday: 138 passengers
Monday: 291 passengers.

From Banff Harbour Station:
There was a special 5am train but only 75 people travelled.
Monday: 460 passengers, only 20 less than 1873; 160 of them got off at Portsoy.

Lesmurdie House in Elgin used to be a small estate, owned by General James Stewart King – who opened up King Street in Elgin, and also owned Newmill. The 1830 built house, existing when John visited, was expanded in 1881. It was split into flats by 2007.

20th July
1874 Mon: At Gordon Castle today. Travelled through the grounds and through Fochabers. Things all looking well at the Castle. A very fine place. Left about 6 o'clock for Banff which we reached about 9pm.

21st July
1874 Tue: Went around the place with the chap that came from the Castle in the morning. Earthed up potatoes in the forenoon. At Alvah Show in the afternoon. A fine day.

22nd July
1874 Wed: Pulling blackcurrants this morning. I stopped at the Orchard today. Cut the weeds among the new grass. Earthed up some potatoes and pinched lateral shoots off the vines. A light shower. Pulling fruit down at the other garden all day.

23rd July
1874 Thu: Pulled blackcurrants this morning and onions. Hoed the most of the day and down bathing at dinnertime. Fine day.

24th July
1874 Fri: Took down a basket of gooseberries this morning, the first of them. Earthed up potatoes etc through the day. Fine day.

25th July
1874 Sat: Pulled a basket of blackcurrants and one of gooseberries and carrots and onions a basket of. Helped Ingram down with them and came home again. Hoed pieces through the garden and came at Kirkside McDuff Artillery. Melvin and Ingram went away to Troup. Fine day.

John obviously made a point of visiting Gordon Castle, using his long weekend. The Castle itself was considerably more extensive than it is today (refer to the note for 2nd January) and there were extensive gardens, both in the front of the House, and also the walled garden a little distance away, built circa 1803 and 4. This is known by many people today since it has been developed by Angus and Zara Gordon Lennox since 2008. The Head Gardener at the time of visit to Gordon Castle was John Webster; we don't know if John would have had an introduction to him from Mr Mackie at Duff House, but John obviously came away from Gordon Castle quite impressed. This photo is from 1903 but would show the flavour of the walled garden as John would have seen it.

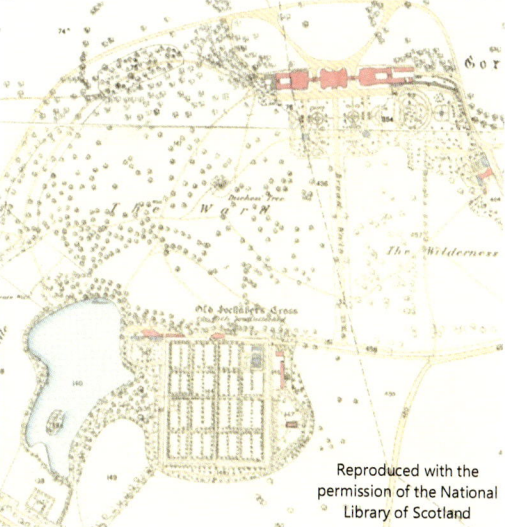

Reproduced with the permission of the National Library of Scotland

Alvah Show – see next page

Macduff Artillery Volunteers were another "Battery" just as were the Banff Artillery Volunteers, all in the Banffshire Garrison. Kirkside being a farm estate about a mile upriver from Banff Bridge on the Macduff side. *See note for 17th April.*

26th July
1874 Sun: Slept with Bagra last night, up in the morning and down to the sea bathing. At the church in the evening. A fine cool day.

27th July
1874 Mon: Sent down a basket of gooseberries and one of blackcurrants today. Earthed up potatoes in the forenoon. Hoeing a little in the afternoon. A fine day.

28th July
1874 Tue: Sent down a basket of blackcurrants and one of gooseberries. Finished earthing up potatoes. Boiled some blackcurrants today. A fine day.

29th July
1874 Wed: Took down a basket of black and goose today. Down at the other garden all day pulling blackcurrants. All forenoon Ingram and me pulled 94lbs of blackcurrants in 2½ hours. Dunged and commenced to dig a piece beside the fruitroom for spinach. A picnic in the Flower Garden today. Very warm.

30th July
1874 Thu: Sent down a basket of onions only today. Commenced to clean the Broad Walk today. Made a boil of red gooseberries in the morning. Pulling blackcurrants all day in the other garden.

31st July
1874 Fri: Down in the morning at the other garden pulling blackcurrants. Took down a basket of gooseberries with us. At this or other the rest of the day. I forgot to mention the rubbish hillock was taken away on Thursday; that was down at the other Bothy. It has been here since the new Vinery went up. Fine day.

The Alvah Show on Tuesday 21st July was the inaugural show for the Alvah Horticultural Society. It was held in a field close to the "romantic Bridge of Alvah", and Lord Fife had given permission for visitors to come through his policies to get there. Busses had been laid on, and most of Alvah and a lot of Banff attended.

There were many classes for flowers, fruit and vegetables, mostly won by amateur gardeners. Prize winners came from as far away as Pathhead, south of Edinburgh, perhaps demonstrating this was not an insubstantial show.

Black and Goose berries presumably – from the Orchard. And then lots of blackcurrants from Airlie Gardens. Although we know where the Fruitroom was in Airlie Gardens (*see Ch 5*), we don't know which of The Orchard buildings was the Fruitroom.

The Flower Garden is what is generally now called Airlie Gardens.

The Broadwalk was at The Orchard, but we don't know which path (*refer to Ch 5*).

At The Orchard, it was mainly vegetables in the upper garden (491);

Mainly fruit in the lower garden (492);

The walled area with a circular path may have been a Flower Garden

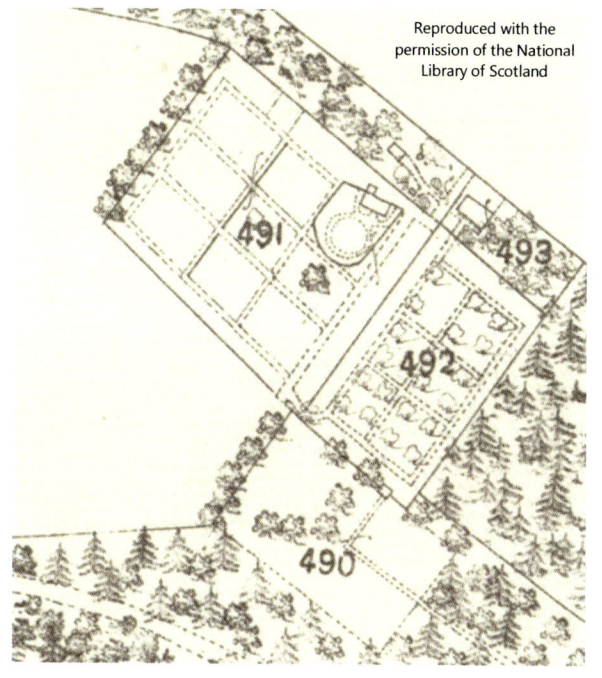

Reproduced with the permission of the National Library of Scotland

1st August
1874 Sat: Sent down a basket of redcurrants and one of carrots today. Hoeing the Broad Walk at the Orchard. Pulling fruit at the other garden. Fine day.

2nd August
1874 Sun: Down at church in the forenoon, hearing Moodie and Sankey. An awful crowd, the half of them did not get in I suppose to the established church. Over at McDuff in the afternoon hearing Sankey but heard little of him, such a crowd and a rough day too. At Duff House Park in the evening after we came out of the church at the usual time, then from the Park to the church again so I was pretty well churched today. Rough today.

3rd August
1874 Mon: Sent down a bagful of apples that the wind blew down. Did not work after that. Went to the church again in the forenoon a short time. Bathed in the afternoon. Had Miss Davidson up a short time in the forenoon. Went home a bit with her. A fine day.

4th August
1874 Tue: Sent down a basket of gooseberries today. Down pulling blackcurrants all day. A fine day.

5th August
1874 Wed: Sent down a basket of gooseberries. At the Orchard but did not do much today as it was raining most of the day.

6th August
1874 Thu: Sent down a basket of gooseberries today for the last of them. Hoeing and scuttering about at one thing or other. A pretty rough day.

Moody and Sankey were big news in Banff and Macduff, they were here for a week, bringing their style of evangelism to Scotland, as part of a tour around the UK. A petition had been signed by many people in Banff, Macduff and Whitehills and a deputation had visited them during their Inverness visit to implore them to include Banff and Macduff. They agreed, but said they were coming "for a rest". They did manage to get some fishing on the river on Sat 1st Aug!

The visit started with a morning service at the Harvest Church, before an 11 o'clock service at Banff Parish Church. As John says, this was very crowded and many hundreds of people could not get in – but up to 2,000 apparently did! At 3 o'clock they had an open-air meeting in Macduff in front of Murray's Institution where a canvas cover had been erected. A thousand people came to this. Murray's Institution was a school from 1848 to 1888, where the Knowes Hotel is today.

The biggest event was held at 7pm, in the Duff House Park. The congregation was larger than anyone ever remembered before. The Banffshire Journal estimated 5,000, but Rev Bruce thinks it was nearer 15,000. Services continued all week, with huge audiences, some coming from as far away as Inverness; every hotel and lodging-house were fully occupied and many came by boat – and slept in them overnight.

Rev Bruce describes Moody as "manly in every sense of the word", with a "well-knit muscular frame and burly appearance". "He was alive in every fibre of his frame; and yet of the every tenderest feeling and susceptibility." "His sympathy and spiritual guidance were every night asked up to late hours."
"Mr Sankey was skilled in this delicate work also. But it was as a singer of hymns that he excelled. I have never heard his equal in moving the heart through the ear." "His pronounciation was so perfect that every word of it told." "The sweetness of the fine baritone voice, combined with a certain manliness of tone and look, simply overpowered the people."

7th August
1874 Fri: Pulling out the rankest of the weeds, out amongst the potatoes. In the upper garden in the forenoon. Mitchell was up in the afternoon so we went down to Banff in the evening. I was at church twice. A fine day.

8th August
1874 Sat: Tossing the Broad Walk at the Orchard today and hoeing most of the narrow ones in the upper garden. Out on the sea in a boat in the evening for the first time in my life. Been a fine day.

9th August
1874 Sun: Down at the sea bathing in the morning and in Deveron. In the forenoon at Eden in the afternoon. Went round by Tarlair with the girls and back again with them and then home. It was morning before Pyper and I got home. A fine day.

10th August
1874 Mon: Sent down a basket of redcurrants today and one of onions. At John Barclay's wife's funeral; she was buried at McDuff. Stopped at the other Bothy for my dinner. Raining from 1 o'clock the rest of the day.

11th August
1874 Tue: Mr Mackie and Ingram away in the morning to the Flower Show at Turriff. Raining the most of the day so I did not get anything done hardly. Mitchell was up in the afternoon, so I went down to Banff with him and got drunk.

12th August
1874 Wed: Pretty dull day again, not doing much. In fact I have hardly done anything for a month back.

Tossing the Broad Walk – a gravel path (*see note for 23rd Jun*) presumably means moving the stones around so that it looks neater – sort of like raking.

John had been out on a boat in the river a couple of times, but obviously 8th August was the first time in his life he had been out to sea. He presumably didn't mind it as by 23rd August he was 3 miles off in a boat fishing!

There were two John Barclay's around Banff in 1874; a farmer at Cowfolds, and a retired doctor on Old Castle Gate. We don't know which one John refers to here.

The Flower Show at Turriff was one of the larger ones in the area (but see also Fyvie two days later). Mr Mackie was the judge "for the professional class", two of the prizes judged being Best Floral Design by Journeymen Gardeners (won for Forglen Gardens) and Best House Bouquet by Apprentice Gardeners (won for Ardmiddle House).

An illustration of a typical Flower Show (from "The Garden Illustrated Weekly Journal", often just referred to as "Garden Illustrated") courtesy of the Biodiversity Heritage Library.

13th August
1874 Thu: Mr Mackie away to Fyvie Flower show today to be a judge; he was that at Turriff. Bagra up tonight pulling some currants to send to Troup. Pretty dull.

14th August
1874 Fri: An awful rough night last night. The herring boats were like to be a cad to airt. There were three or four cad to splinters at Macduff harbour and they say there was one sunk in the Bay. Keeping sticks into my Vinery some today as I have no coals down at the harbour. At dinnertime some herring bought and we were through to skin before we came to the harbour. An awful day.

15th August
1874 Sat: Sent down a barrowful of carrots and onions today. Pinched the young shoots of the vines today and some small jobs. A fine day.

16th August
1874 Sun: Down bathing in the morning. One of our company very near drowned. Webster went in to a deep place and could not get out again till Alex Smith went to the rescue and I went in and helped him out. Down looking through Duff House in the forenoon. Not at church today. A fine day.

17th August
1874 Mon: Sent down a basket of redcurrants and some red gooseberries. Hoeing the currant border in the forenoon. Went down to the other Bothy for my dinner. Went to the Smithy with my scythe in the afternoon. After that stopped and helped them off with the nets off the strawberries. Mr Mackie hoed his winter onions today. A fine day. Shot a cat.

18th August
1874 Tue: Pulled the first of the French beans today. Cut a lot of cabbage to clear a piece for sowing winter onions. I sowed two beds today. A fine day.

The Fyvie Flower Show was a full Agricultural Show with the Flower Show being a much smaller part. Only farmers from within the parish of Fyvie were allowed to enter. The Banffshire Journal commented "it is safe to say that very few, if any, sections of the country of the same extent could produce such a fine show of cattle and horses".

Friday 14th August 1874 was a particularly awful day for weather "a violent storm, accompanied with unusually heavy rainfall. The wind from N.E. blew with the force of a gale for several hours, reaching it's height between nine and ten o'clock in the morning. The sea was very much disturbed, and … the fleet of herring boats suffered severely in the storm." (from Banffshire Journal).

The weather on Thursday evening was good and upwards of a hundred boats proceeded to sea, some going three and a half hours distance and shot their nets. At about midnight the fishermen became alarmed, but they thought the wind would ease, but by four in the morning the "tempest burst in full fury". Some boats pulled their nets, others had to drop them. The first boats got in to Macduff between five and six before the tide had fully ebbed, but those later couldn't get in for want of water, and had to lie perilously exposed outside the harbour until about nine o'clock.

Macduff Harbour in about 1870

The *"Ocean Queen"* from Macduff was the first dashed upon the rocks, shortly followed by a Banff boat, then a Portessie boat. "Cad to airt" as John describes them, smashed to pieces. Another Portessie boat, the *"Jessie Ann"* capsized at sea with the loss of five men. A total of 150 boats crammed into Macduff harbour that day. Similar instances took place all along the coast.

See the note for 7th May about the Smithy.

19th August
1874 Wed: Up about four o'clock today. Commenced to cut the flower garden taking off the grass in the forenoon and cutting strawberries in the afternoon; cutting the runners of them you know. A fine day.

20th August
1874 Thu: Up early today again cutting grass. Taking it off in the forenoon and cutting the edges etc. Among the strawberries in the afternoon cutting the runners of them. A fine day.

21st August
1874 Fri: Up early cutting grass again, clearing it off in the forenoon. Raking off the straw out among the strawberries in the afternoon and taking it away to the wood. A fine day.

22nd August
1874 Sat: Down at the other gardens today hoeing the strawberries and raking them. Got them all cleaned. Did not finish the cutting today for some mistake about taking away the grass. A fine day. Had a terrible night with the Eden chaps. Two of them got a little beered over at Macduff and Banff together. Up in the Gallowhill before we got home. An awful night - most terrible.

23rd August
1874 Sun: Up about 9 o'clock. Mitchell was up all night. Took our breakfast and cleaned ourselves. Went down and saw through the House in the forenoon and I was down a while in the afternoon. At church in the evening. A fine day.

24th August
1874 Mon: Pulled french beans but I believe I should not have done it. Hoeing the rest of the day at the Orchard. Down at dinnertime. Had a bath. A fine day.

Eden House and estate had been developed in the earlier 1800s by James Cunningham Grant Duff, a distant cousin of James 5th Earl Fife. It had extensive gardens, including the present walled garden.

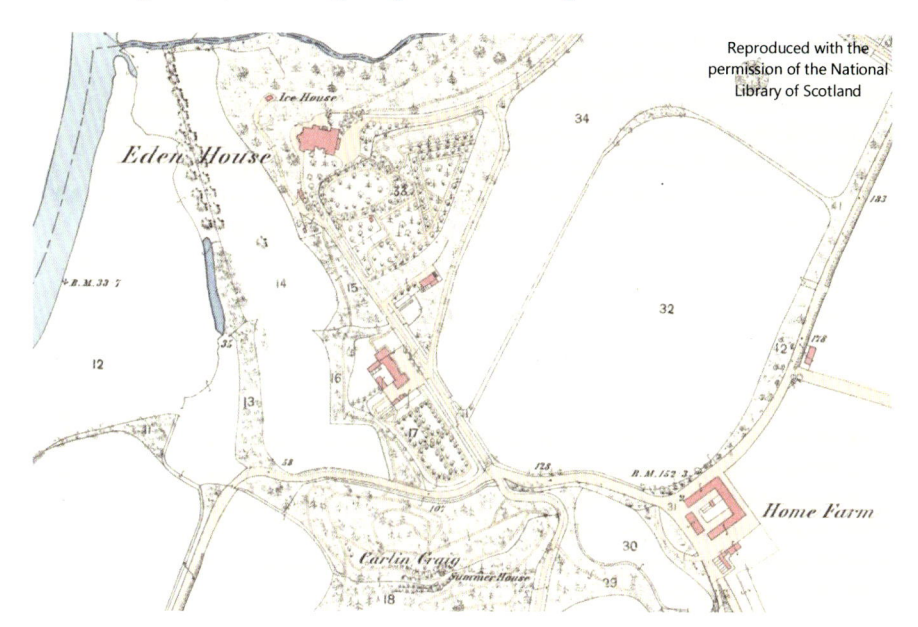

Reproduced with the permission of the National Library of Scotland

On this occasion it was the chaps from Eden, perhaps as a result of John visiting them on 9th Aug. It seems a friendship developed, particularly with one guy he calls Smith, and he meets up with either the chaps and/or girls from Eden many times (20th, 26th, 27th Sep; 17th, 22nd & 25th Oct).

In the later 20th century the gardens had been left to grow wild, but the ones near the house have now had attention from new owners, and the walled garden by Banff Day Services.

The employees were obviously allowed to look through Duff House when the Earl was not there; even some of the Eden girls did on 20th Sep. *See note for 30th Aug.*

25th August
1874 Tue: Sent down a barrowful of cabbage and some onions. Hoeing weeds out amongst the potatoes etc. J Mitchell was up in the afternoon. Was out in a boat in the evening catching fish about 3 miles off. A fine day.

26th August
1874 Wed: Some carrots and onions sent down today. Holling out Dante Lions out of the Walks and commenced to hoe round the edges among the gooseberries. They were pulling some of the earliest apples down in the other garden today. A fine day.

27th August
1874 Thu: Down finishing the flower garden cutting. Took down 4 basketful of Codlin apples at breakfastime. Hoeing among the gooseberries in the afternoon. A fine day, but a good shower.

28th August
1874 Fri: Sent down some onions and carrots. Hoeing in the low half at the Orchard. A fine day.

29th August
1874 Sat: Did not do much today. Raining most of the day. Down at Deveron fishing a good while. Ingram came home and went away to Troup at dinnertime, and Bagra.

30th August
1874 Sun: Slept down with Mil*** last night. Mr Lemon and Mitchell was up today and down at the House looking at the stuffed birds. At church in the evening. A fine day.

31st August
1874 Mon: Down at the other garden today. Raining in the morning but cleared up. I was clipping the hedge before the Bothy door today. Bagra and some of them was pricking out some Sweet Williams into beds. Ingram's brother was here last night. A fine day.

Holling = excavating. Seemingly not a common Scots word and only a few examples known, one being in the Annals of Banff, Vol 2, p64, in 1695 "Delated .... some of John Leel's children for holling a bees' byke upon the Sabbath day". Also used by John on 9th Sep.
"Delated" means "admonished" and a bees' byke is a bees' nest.

Codlin is an old English term for a green cooking apple. A most common variety of Codlin apples was the Keswick Codlin; this variety can still be easily bought as a tree today. So called Keswick because it was found in about 1790 behind a wall at Gleaston Castle by John Sanders, a nurseryman in Keswick who propagated it.
It is a generally a heavy cropper; note on 5th Sep John took five basketfuls down to Duff House.

Duff House used to have a collection of stuffed birds and animals that were on display by 1903 in what today is the shop on the ground floor, but was originally designated a "Common Hall" – the ground floor originally being intended for servants. In 1903 (by Mrs K Warren Clouston written up in "The Connoisseur") these were described as "cases of rare birds and trophies of the chase adorn the walls."

Some of these trophies were more fully described in 1845 by James Imlach, in that Lower Vestibule, as "various horns of the red or highland deer" which had come from Marr Lodge. Also, in the Drawing Room – 2nd floor – were indeed some rare birds:
- the Capercaillie both cock and hen;
- an interesting species of Grouse, formally abundant in Scotland (of which the 4th Earl had imported many living specimens from Norway, some of which have been kept alive and in good health for years, in an adjoining aviary, where they have brought forth young;
- a stuffed specimen of the real Highland Wild Cat, from Marr Lodge;
- specimens of the Black Cock and Grey Hen;
- Ptarmigan in its winter, in its autumnal and it's summer plumage;
- Common Red Grouse, "found in no other part of the world except Great Britain."

1st September
1874 Tue: Took down French beans and some tomatoes this morning. Pulling apples and pears all day. An awful shower and a strong breeze about the middle of the day that sent down a great many of them. Old Losan was in a terrible state about some Jargonelles we ate.

2nd September
1874 Wed: Pulled the first of the strawberry pippins today. Took down about two baskets of them. Pulled rasps and then went down to the long border and pulled weeds. It came on a good shower and we was forced to leave and cut the verges. Cleaned up.

3rd September
1874 Thu: Took down a hurleyful of potatoes today. For the first raked the grass of the edges of the Canal Walk and commenced to hoe it. Howed and raked past the Canal door. Down in the evening to the thrashing mill. A fine day.

4th September
1874 Fri: Took down another hurleyful of potatoes and some cabbage and a bagful of apples that was in the loft. Hoed and raked the Canal Walk and commenced to hoe the flower garden walks. A fine day but some good showers.

5th September
1874 Sat: Took down 5 baskets of Codlin apples in the morning. Hoed and raked the Walks in the flower garden but it came on rain so we did not get them finished. Rained mostly all afternoon.

6th September
1874 Sun: Gerrard came up in the morning with the long coal. Jock written, got word written to get to meet a girl down in the direction of Troup but did not go. At church in the evening. A fine day.

Jargonelles – pears – is one of the oldest varieties in cultivation. There may have been some in The Orchard, but we do know that a lot of the original south wall of Airlie Gardens had some old Jargonelles trees that were retained when the Gardens were developed in about 1860. This wall was removed when New Road was built in 1965, if not before. These old trees are said to have borne "loads of luscious pears".

There was also a "Bon Chrétien" pear tree, "whose weight of fruit was sometimes phenomenal; now also gone.

Mahood (in his 1919 book "Banff and District") claims that many of the pear trees had been introduced to Banff by the Carmelite monks.

Strawberry pippin apples. *See note opposite 14th and 15th Sep.*

Codlin apples. *See note for 27th Aug.*

We are not sure what John means by "long coal" but his writing is quite clear. John and James Gerrard were Cartwrights and hence presumably why one of them brought the coal – ready for winter both for where the gardeners lived and for the Vinery.

7th September
1874 Mon: Two bobbies up at us today about apples; got a few. Hoeing and raking before the Bothy door. Finished the flower garden walks and started the kitchen. Duncan up at us in the evening for shooting. A very duff day.

8th September
1874 Tue: Hoeing and rolling walks in the kitchen garden today. Took down a hurleyful of potatoes in the morning. A pretty dull day.

9th September
1874 Wed: Holling potatoes and cleaning them. Making ready for the Show. Commenced to put in cuttings today of Bijou. A very rainy day.

10th September
1874 Thu: Down in the morning making up bouquets for the Show. Took down carrots, currants, gooseberries etc from the Orchard. Preparing for the Show.

11th September
1874 Fri: Banff Show today. Carried up our produce in the morning. Got a fine quiet day although some heavy showers. A good [day]; we had about 39 prizes, 19 Firsts, 18 Seconds and the rest Thirds.

12th September
1874 Sat: The young Mackies came up this morning to pick apples. Took down 5 basketfuls. Putting in cuttings the rest of the day - Trentham Rose and Tom Thumb. Dull today, showers.

13th September
1874 Sun: Up at the Bridge of Alvah in the forenoon. Bagra and Mitchell and me did not go to church today; was too late this hit. A fine day.

Bobbies must mean the same today, policeman (after Robert Peel who established the police in 1829). In 1874 the Police were based on the ground floor of the "Council Buildings", which is the Court House today (Low St), built in 1871. The building occupied today by the police was built as the Commercial Bank of Scotland in about 1865.

The photo is one of the twenty or so policemen in the Banffshire Constabulary in 1874 (but not a Sergeant at that time).

Reproduced by kind permission of British Police History and John Green

Duff. Although the Earl's Fife family surname was originally Duff, the use of the word "duff" to mean a useless or bad or wrong thing or person had a different derivation. Duff used to be an old Scots word for buttock.

The surname Duff is apparently derived from the Gaelic "Dubh" meaning dark or black, and used to be used as a term for a dark haired man.

DUFF more recently – since a film in 1995 - is a rude term as Designated Ugly Fat Friend, intended to be used to describe someone that makes the user look better.

Holling, excavating; *see note for 26th Aug.*

Bijou geraniums; *see note for 17th Mar.*

The **Banff Show** was the third show of the Banffshire Horticultural Association, a prosperous and growing organisation. It was held in the grounds of Banff Castle courtesy of Mr Sinclair. The show of flowers, fruit and vegetables was apparently excellent, with professional exhibits from Duff House, Troup, Netherdale, Craigston, Park, Eden, Ardmiddle, Montcoffer and others.

The display of flowers was very fine, and the marigolds, dahlias, picotees (carnations) and gladioli came in for particular praise.

In the fruit, the two that had a lot of praise were Jargonnel pears from Mr Scotland of the Commercial Bank, and "the grapes from Duff House worthily attracted much attention" carrying off the first prizes in both classes. Mr Mackie of Duff House was also praised for his bouquet of skill and taste.

Trentham Rose geraniums; *see note for 12th Nov.*

Geranium **Tom Thumb** is another variety that was considered old even in 1873, but still one that "should be retained in every garden" (Journal of Horticulture 1872). It was scarlet, dwarf and compact, and bloomed all summer.

14th September
1874 Mon: Holled potatoes in the morning, carrots and onions. Took them down in the Hurley. Went back again to pull apples; pulled them all but the Hawthornden. But it came on rain so we did not get them all taken down. Putting in cuttings of all the different varieties of geraniums, some verbenas etc. Raining most of the day.

15th September
1874 Tue: Took down a hurleyful of potatoes and two big basketfuls of egg apples which we did not get down yesterday. Putting in cuttings of verbenas, heliotrope, cuphia, senecia, viola and pansies. Came home sooner than usual and took up some onions and spread them out. A fine day.

16th September
1874 Wed: Took down a hurleyful of potatoes. The foreman and Bagra was trenching the small border at the back of the Hotel that was strawberries. Ingram and I went and holled some potatoes that was in a field, clearing it for cabbage. I came home at dinnertime to pull onions. Dull day.

17th September
1874 Thu: Took down a hurleyful of potatoes this morning. Wheeled dung to a field we are going to dig for cabbage then went to the canal border and hoed chickweed till dinnertime. Then we earthed up celery for the first time except for the Show. It came on a shower as I came home. Raw day.

18th September
1874 Fri: Had nothing to take down today. Put on a frame on some new dung they had got in last night to strike verbenas on. After that we went to the Canal border and hoed it. Then took out the cabbage plants that was beside the Little Vinery. I hoed the place. Fine day. Mr Mackie at Aberdeen Show today.

The Hawthornden was a cooking apple, still available today, with a delicate pink flush. However it's skin was very easily bruised, and this meant it was not suitable for long distance transport, so it's popularity died out after the nineteenth century.

Crow Egg Apples are round but flattened, with a pale yellow or green or both, skin, with red blushes. The finely textured flesh is white, crisp, tended and juicy. As a dessert apple the flesh is somewhat swet. 
The "Northern Crow Egg Apple" was first described in a Herbal (combination of a botanical and medical) book, "Theatrum Botanicum" by John Parkinson in 1640.

Strawberry pippin *See 2ⁿᵈ Sep.*

These eating apples are red-striped with a pleasant crunch and a pleasing mostly sweet with limited tart flavour. The skin is however quite tough. Various varieties readily available.

The Aberdeen Show was held in the Music Hall. Mr Mackie was one of the judges for Pot Plants and Fruit.

19th September
1874 Sat: Had nothing to take down today. Dug the field for cabbage in the forenoon. I hoed about the back of the Hotel in the afternoon. Dull day. Bagra and Ingram went to Troup today.

20th September
1874 Sun: Slept with Melvin last night. Rose in the morning and went down and bathed with Smith and Pyper. A very good bath. They were up in the forenoon [with] two of the Eden chaps and two of the girls was over the afternoon looking through the place. Then we went to the Catholic Chapel and went out road with them. A fine day.

21st September
1874 Mon: Took down a hurleyful of potatoes, some carrot and onions. Hoed the rasps in the forenoon and it came on rain. We picked withered leaves and cut shreds etc. I came home after dinnertime. Cut some shanked grapes off etc. Very rainy night.

22nd September
1874 Tue: Took down French beans today. Got our scythes and came up to the Rosery and cut it. Raked it off and finished it in the afternoon. Fine day.

23rd September
1874 Wed: Holled a hurleyful of potatoes. Young Mackie came up with baskets for plums and the last of the apples; we pulled about 60lbs of plums. Mackie came up and helped us down with them. Hoed strawberries in the forenoon etc. Planted cabbage in the afternoon for next season use. A fine day.

24th September
1874 Thu: Took down a hurleyful of carrots today. Pulled them all and took down with me two baskets of apples that we pulled yesterday. Have to make our meet ourselves now we gave Mungo the kick yesterday. Hoeing the canal border today. A fine day.

The Hotel is the Fife Arms Hotel. *See note for 5th Feb 1874.*

Catholic Chapel. *See note for 29th Mar 1874.*

A shanked grape is where individual berries in a bunch fail to develop their colour. They ultimately shrivel and look more like a raisin. The stalks turn black and wither, which gives rise to the term. It can be caused by too much, or too little, watering, but also if it is cropped too vigourously too quickly.

Montcoffer *See 25th Oct*

There is both the Manor House of Montcoffer, and the Mains of Montcoffer as a farm; both are substantial and both had laid out gardens. There is also a formal nursery at Montcoffer, as part of the Duff House estate. The Honourable George Skene Duff, younger brother of James the 5th Earl Fife, was living in Montcoffer House, but the tenant in the Earl Fife owned farm is not known. In earlier times Montcoffer House was the home of William Rose, the Factor to the Duff Estate in the time of James 2nd Earl, and where many of the huge collection of Duff papers were kept until they were moved to Aberdeen University Library.

Reproduced with the permission of the National Library of Scotland

25th September
1874 Fri: Took down 2 basketfuls of Damson Plums today, 20lb each. Hoeing the rest of the day in the kitchen garden. A no bad day.

26th September
1874 Sat: Hoed some before the Vinery in the morning among the vegetable marrows, thinned out some of them. Tossing today in the kitchen garden the thing we hoed before. I came home short after dinnertime and took in onions at the orchard. Over at Macduff in the evening with some of the Eden chaps and up at Mutton Bells before we went home.

27th September
1874 Sun: Up today and went to the church of Alvah. Met Smith there, went to his fathers, then to Eden. Had a fine promenade with the girls; some tired out before I got home. A hot day.

28th September
1874 Mon: Rose about 9 o'clock today. Hoeing all day in the flower garden. Came home and took up the rest of the onions into the loft. A fine day.

29th September
1874 Tue: Took down a hurleyful of potatoes, some French beans. Dug a small piece and planted a bed of young strawberry plants, Myatts seedling, and some young brussel sprouts. Goldsworth and Duncan in the garden shooting rabbits. Came home after dinner and pulled damson plums. A fine day but a good rain towards evening.

30th September
1874 Wed: Pulled the last of the damsons in the morning and took them down. Pulling out the worst of the weeds through the garden among the potatoes etc. Commenced to take up the seed potatoes. Pulled the last of the apples at the potato shed and the large iron pier at the back of the Hotel. Fine day.

Damsons are relatively small plum-like fruit, often with deep blue skins, with quite an astringent taste. Often used in jam making, and said to be more hardier trees.

The Mutton Bells most likely was a pub in Macduff, but no record can be found.

Joseph Myatt,, died 1855 was a market gardener and pioneer of strawberry growing. He was based in Camberwell in Surrey, and then later moved to Deptford. He really did pioneer the strawberry as generally in the early eighteen hundreds only the very small wild ones were eaten. Myatt developed larger fruits and he became very successful.

The most famous strawberry ever, developed by Myatt in 1841, was "British Queen". Large fruit, sometimes very large, roundish, flattened, and cockscomb shaped, the smaller fruit ovate or conical. Skin pale red, colouring unequal, being frequently white or greenish -white at the apex. Flesh white, firm, juicy, and with a remarkably rich and exquisite flavour. It has led to many other related varieties.

The list of Myatt's varieties did not include any called "Myatts Seedling" so presumably John was planting seedlings of a Myatt variety:

    Myatt's Pine
    Myatt's Eliza;
    British Queen;
    Prince Albert;
    Deptford Pine.

These heritage varieties do not seem to be available today, but they paved the way for many other cultivars.

William Goldsworth was the Head Gamekeeper on the Duff House estate.

1st October
1874 Thu: Slept in today, down at breakfastime. Taking up seed potatoes all day. We had two women gathering. Paid today I got 5 pounds 17 shillings and had 7 shillings taken up before, and besides that I got one pound in a present for thinning and attending the grapes well. A fine day.

2nd October
1874 Fri: Slept in today. Pulled the black **** pears today. Filled up the blanks in the cabbage that the rabbits made. Earthed up some cauliflower because the wind was tossing them. Bought a pair of ready made trousers tonight for 14/6. Been a very rough day.

3rd October
1874 Sat: Putting in cuttings of calceolarias today all day. Put in all the varieties that we have, some senecio. Wet dull kind of day.

4th October
1874 Sun: Rose about 10 o'clock today. Down and got some rabbit broth. Was down at the Brewery with my uncle. Went up and got my tea. I went to church, Mr Bruce preaching. Very cold and rough.

5th October
1874 Mon: Weeding edges all day in the kitchen garden. Took back the new trousers that I bought on Friday night and got them changed for another pair which I think will fit. Cold.

6th October
1874 Tue: Pricked out some red cabbage into a bed. Pruning hedges a while till it came on rain the we put in cuttings of senecio and allysum varieties. I planted in half a frame of cauliflower for spring. Cutting the grass in the wood and between the Bothy and the shrubs. Dull wet day. I have got a terrible dose of cold.

This is John's fourth pay day during his apprenticeship; this time he was paid £5 17s; 4 shillings more than three months ago – excluding his extras. The bonus of £1 for looking after the grapes – and he clearly must have done that well as they won both the prizes in the Banff Show (see note for 11th Sep) – must have been a welcome extra.

Black pears used to be quite common, and are believed to have been brought to Britain by the Romans. They are often known as Black Worcester Pears, because Queen Elizabeth 1st is said to have seen on a visit to Worcester in 1575; and ever since three pears appear on Worcester's coat of arms.

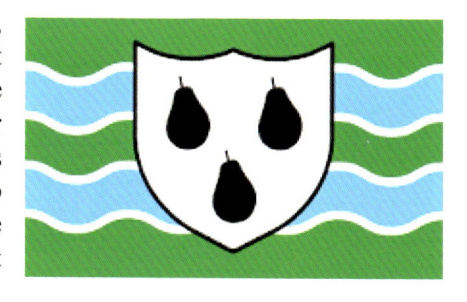

Black pear trees can be particularly high, reaching over 15 metres (50 feet). The pears are not really black, but darker skinned than other varieties. They were not typically eaten fresh, but they had long storage capabilities (up to 4 to 7 months in a cool dark place) and therefore were used a lot in baking.

They are not grown commercially today but can be obtained from specialist nurseries.

7th October
1874 Wed: Finished the two beds of onions weeding them this morning. Up at the rosery this forenoon, hoeing and digging down the weeds. Hardly finished when it came on rain just about dinnertime. Making shreds a short time after dinner. Cleaned the walk from the fruitroom and came home after dinner, A wet dull afternoon.

8th October
1874 Thu: Cleaning onions in the morning. Pricked out cauliflower into cold frames all day. The foreman was pruning the hedges and other two was weeding edges etc. No that ill a day.

9th October
1874 Fri: Planting celery, least pricking it out to the foot of the apricot dyke. Hoed the walk by the foot of the wall and raked it in the afternoon. Mackie was up at the Orchard today. A fine day.

10th October
1874 Sat: Hoeing walks in the kitchen garden in the forenoon and earthing up celery [against the] wind. Down to the photographer's after dinner; the rest got themselves taken but we did not get [in] the group because we was getting a hurl to Troup, so we took the hurl. Rather a fine day.

11th October
1874 Sun: At Troup today down at the gardens in the forenoon and round by the braes. Took two rabbits among the rocks. Over at the Wrights and Miss Stephen's in the afternoon. Home by 8 o'clock some tired. A fine day.

12th October
1874 Mon: Commenced to hoe the Broad Walk at the Orchard this morning. Hoeing before the Bothy and some of the walk in the kitchen garden in the forenoon. Raining in the afternoon, cutting shreds and drawing some straw for the potatoes. Cold, dull.

On 31st Dec John and some other gardeners got their CDV – Carte de Visite – photos – taken. John also received two from young ladies that he records in his Diary (*see note for 26th Mar; also 5th Nov*). There had been a plan for another visit to the photographers on 10th Oct, but it seems on this occasion, John's plans for his future career, being able to study another garden were more important to him. At this stage, a month before, he must also have known that he was moving on and this may be his last chance.

A hurl is a ride, a lift in a vehicle.

The Troup House of 1874 is not the Troup House – now a school – of today; nor was it in the same position as the present Troup House. Mr Garden Campbell had the House. Apparently "a large, heavy looking building", as described in 1858 when it had been unoccupied for a number of years. By 1874 it presumably was occupied as his fellow Duff House gardeners had been sent to it (eg 29th Aug) and various fruit and veg had been picked and sent to Troup House.

According to this 1869 map there were three walled garden areas, all of them the other side of the burn to the House itself. Remnants of at least one are visible today.

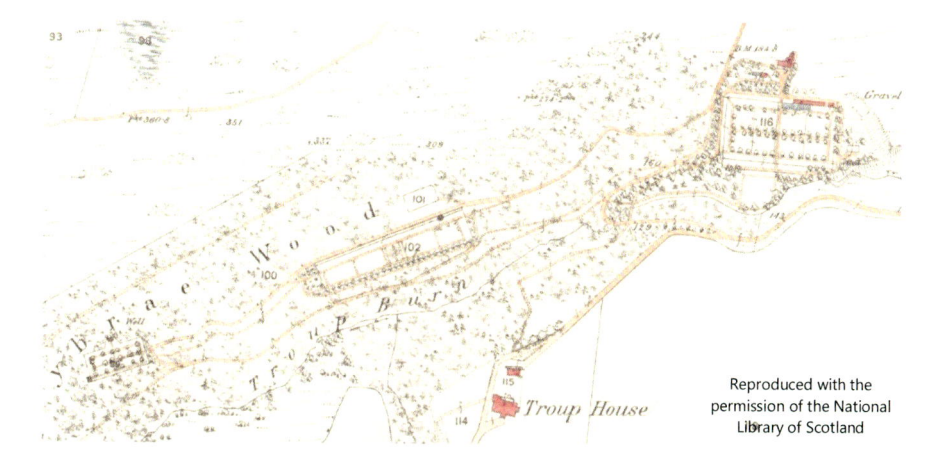

Reproduced with the permission of the National Library of Scotland

Page 187

13th October
1874 Tue: Down in the morning going over the long strabs of grass in the flower garden. Cut the half of the garden, then cut the edges and raked it up. Hoeing kitchen garden walk in the afternoon. A pretty good day.

14th October
1874 Wed: Down in the morning cutting grass. After breakfast tossed some walks in the kitchen garden that was hoed before. Cleaned up the grass in the flower garden till dinnertime, then hoed and raked walks in the Kitchen Garden. Mr Mackie was up at the Orchard and cut some grapes, the first of them cut this year here. A fine day.

15th October
1874 Thu: Taking up potatoes at the Orchard today. Had 3 extra women helping us. Took them all up but some Prince Regents and Early Forties. Mackie was not up today. A fine day but a slight shower.

16th October
1874 Fri: Taking up the rest of the potatoes in the morning. Melvin and Bagra was up after breakfast. We hoed walks in the Flower Garden all the rest of the day. A fine day.

17th October
1874 Sat: Hoeing and rolling the walks in the Flower Gardens. Finished them. Took down a hurleyful of potatoes in the morning. Saw some of the Eden chaps at night. Was up at Gallowhill. A fine day.

18th October
1874 Sun: Rose about 11 o'clock. Dressed myself and went out [to] the Bridge [of Alvah?] but back and shut the Vinery and back to Church. Nothing in particular today. A fine day.

19th October
1874 Mon: Raining in the morning. Cutting shreds in the forenoon, the most of it. Threw up and cleaned in about the vegetable hillocks up in the woods. Down at the Fruitroom. Cleared up some by afternoon.

A strab is a long stalk, in this case of grass. John refers to the Flower Garden, now Airlie Gardens.

John only names two varieties of potato in his Diary, even though he says there were forty varieties grown.
Prince Regent was a variety of merit prior to 1841 and became extremely popular. It was used by many potato breeders and in consequence is found in the pedigree of most of the present day varieties.

The photo is actually of British Queen potatoes, but potatoes had many synonyms, and lists of some of these have been put together, showing, at least in 1894 that British Queen and Prince Regent were the same, just different names by different growers.
One of the main Scottish potato growers and breeders was Alexander Findlay of Auchtermuchty. From all the suppliers in Scotland he seems the most likely to have supplied to Duff House.

No reference in any lists of potatoes can be found to "Early Forties". It may be a synonym of Fortyfold 1836, another of Alexander Findlay's potatoes.

When John says he was up at Gallowhill – the road, there is no known pub there! But it may be he was referring to the actual hill, and not the road. The ascent from Duff House to Gallow Hill, also used to be known as Whin Hill, is not too steep and it used to a popular place for walks because the views from the top were all encompassing. It was so popular that seats had been placed at various points. The Cemetery was started in 1862 but Bellevue Road and where the Academy now is and all the houses around it was all open ground.

Shreds are willow twigs, used for basket making. *See note for 17th Feb.*

20th October
1874 Tue: Put in more earth on the pit in the wood. Finished hoeing and raking the Kitchen Garden Walks. Howed the most of the Canal Walk and raked as much of it as we could. Dull day.

21st October
1874 Wed: Most awful rough day, a real hurricane and raining too. Broke down several trees between this and the other garden. Did very little today but some shreds. At drill in the evening.

22nd October
1874 Thu: Fast day today. Went up to Turriff with the 12 train. Came back with the 4 and off at King Edward and down to Eden then to Netherwood and had some dancing and singing and from that to Macduff and got pretty tight. Came home about 1 o'clock, An awful rough and stormy day. It has been awful rough for two days back.

23rd October
1874 Fri: The weather is more settled today. Finishing the cleaning of the Canal Walk in the forenoon. Commenced to prick out the last frame of cauliflower in the afternoon but did not finish it as Bagra and Ingram hoeing shit for the peas.

24th October
1874 Sat: Taking up the last of the potatoes, some later kinds, in the forenoon. Taking up carrots, beet and parsnips and putting them in the afternoon. Cutting down some of the herbaceous plans in the Flower Border and taking them away. Fine day.

25th October
1874 Sun: Had artichokes for dinner today. It cleared in the evening; went out the road with Smith from Eden. Met in with two country quines, went to Montcoffer with them and got milk and bread and came home by the Bridge of Alvah.

On Wed 21st Oct John calls the wind a real hurricane. The Banffie reports the occurrence as follows:

> In Banff "the gale commenced very suddenly, about nine o'clock. The wind had been from the south, and, in a very short time, veered round to west-north-west. The sea was very disturbed, and the rain and spray, blown from the crests of the waves, shortened the range of vision seawards. Fortunately, none of the fishing boats belonging to the port were at sea."
> "The force of the wind below over some of the herring-boats stationed on the Green Banks, but none of them were injured. In the streets, during the space of an hour, it was difficult to walk, as well as unsafe from the quantity of slates falling off the roofs of houses. Some of the older and more exposed houses were a good deal damaged, a number of chimney cans were thrown down, and the rain found its way into may houses from the force with which it was driven by the wind."

Most of Scotland experienced this wind and damage was widespread.

See note for 2nd April explaining a Fast Day – fasting in preparation for taking the sacrament – holy communion, which was only twice a year.

Netherwood (today Netherwood Farm) was a substantial building with gardens. It is east of Eden, just off the A947, where in 1877 Robert Williamson was farming. The 1868 map calls it "Funkieston" but by 1902 The Ordnance Survey clearly has it as Netherwood.

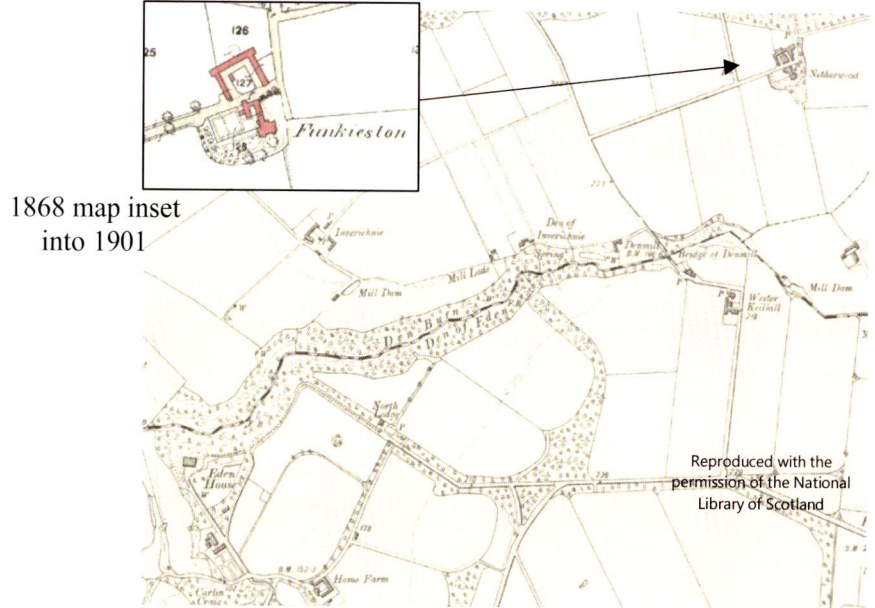

1868 map inset into 1901

Reproduced with the permission of the National Library of Scotland

Montcoffer. See note on page opposite 21st Sep.

26th October
1874 Mon: Put on some earth on the seed pit in the morning and after breakfast we was at the Canal Border pulling and hoeing the roughest of the weeds. Filling up blanks among the cabbage and taking the best plants out of the seed beds and putting them in a bed by themselves and hoeing the beds which they were in. A fine day.

27th October
1874 Tue: Cut some willows at the top of the onion brake and forked out some weeds in the morning. Pruning raspberries all the rest of the day and tying them up. A fine day.

28th October
1874 Wed: Up at the Orchard today trenching the onion brake and dunging it. Did not finish it today we will likely be at it tomorrow. A fine day.

29th October
1874 Thu: Finished trenching the brake at the Orchard; took us to about 12 o'clock. After that cleaning the boxes of geranium cuttings and taking them out of the frames into the Houses then lifted the frames to their winter quarters. Had a bit of a row with Duncan. A fine day.

30th October
1874 Fri: Down opening the Ice House this morning. The rest of the day we was raking leaves among the shrubbery and through the grass about the top of the Flower Garden. Mr and Mrs Mackie up at the Orchard this afternoon. Fine quiet day.

31st October
1874 Sat: Raking leaves all day out among the shrubbery and through the Flower Garden. Lord Fife came today. A fine day.

Grape growing (see multiple references)

The vineyard that provided the grapes for the new Vinery at Duff House was the Tweed Vineyards in Clovenfolds in the Tweed valley in the Scottish Borders. It had been started by William Thomson in 1869, covering about 5 acres.

80 years later and his grandson presented a paper to the world "Eighty Years of Grape Growing". This lays out the steps that should be taken throughout the year. Below is a summary of those steps tagged with the dates of the Duff House gardeners actions. This paper also identifies that the vines sent out in 1872 were of the variety "Duke of Buccleuch", named after William's previous employer, a white grape, handsome and richly flavoured – although it has very thin skins. Whether the existing vines at The Orchard are this variety is not so certain.

- paring the bark (24th Jan and 7th Feb);
- thorough cleaning of the Vinery (4th Feb);
- re-doing the drainage inside and out (5th Feb);
- top dressing inside and out (21st and 23rd Feb);
- start heating (23rd Feb); NB start at 45/50°F, increase 5°F each 10 days;
- thorough watering (2nd Mar, 21st Mar, 31st Mar, 18th Apr, 9th May);
- disbudding and pinching out (8th May – in Diary on 10th);
- thinning bunches (6th, 9th, 11th, 29th, 30th Jun, 3rd, 4th Jul);
- ventilate when temp gets to 75°F (13th Jun);
- stop lateral shoots (22nd Jul, 15th Aug);
- syringing to wash out the seedless berries (no mention);
- remove shanked grapes (21st Sep);
- harvest bit by bit (11th Sep, 14th Oct);
- complete harvest may not be until Christmas (5th Nov).

All in all John's Diary provides an excellent record of how vines and grapes should be looked after. There are of course many other aspects, and William Thomson (grandson) stresses that even a few hours of the wrong conditions can ruin a complete crop.

1st November
1874 Sun: Slept down at the other Bothy last night. Bagra and Ingram away at Troup. Killed a squirrel with a stone. I suppose the most important work I did today. Not at Church today. A fine day.

2nd November
1874 Mon: Raining dribbly kind of a day. Worked among the plants and made stakes etc. Lord Macduff came today.

3rd November
1874 Tue: Some rainy kind in the morning but it went over. Took the bad potatoes out of the shed; separated the godly from the unjust and put them into the pit. Made up some blanks among the rasps. Ingram got his leave today.

4th November
1874 Wed: Rowing up mould from a sweet hillock in the wood to the rasps. Spread it then dug or commenced to dig them. Bagra attending the House; Gentry out shooting today and yesterday. 1 dozen plants for the table came today from Cockers Nurserymen in Aberdeen. A fine day.

5th November
Thu: James Melvin left this morning with the first train. Digging among the rasps today. Got a C.D.V. of Miss Stephen. A dull day.

"**separated the godly from the unjust**" is a phrase not heard in today's potato world, but considered to be very expressive. If just one unjust, eg rotten, potato is put into a potato pit or clamp, it can ruin many others around it. So sorting the good ones from the bad ones is very worthwhile task, and this expression sums it up nicely. *Refer to note for 31st Oct 1873 for a potato pit.*

Mould is compost; in this case perhaps leaf mould as it came out of the wood. The RHS advises the best – and quickest - leaf mould comes from oak, beach or hornbeam. Sweet – good – leaf mould can take at least two years, which of course can happen naturally in the woods.

Cockers was, and is, a nursery in Aberdeen, that started in 1840 by the great, great grandfather of the present senior partner. James Cocker had been the head gardener at Castle Fraser but apparently quarrelled with his employer who wanted him to pick fruit on a Sunday. It started as a nursery focussing on forest trees and herbaceous plants. Unfortunately they do not have any records back to 1874. Today they focus on roses.

Miss **Stephen** appears five times in this Diary (17th & 20th Mar, 11th Oct, 5th Nov).
In March John fills, and "puts way to" a bag of mould to her; this sounds a bit contradictory to him receiving her **CDV** – carte de visite – on 5th Nov. We have not been able to identify which of the many female Stephens in Gamrie that she may have been. *See 26th Mar for an example of a CDV.*

> **Slacks of Tipperty** (see 8th Nov) is the hill on the Aberchirder Road (A97) after the Alvah turning, before the B road junction towards Montblairy and Turriff. The area is now farmland but in John's time it was wooded on both sides with walks.
>
> Reproduced with the permission of the National Library of Scotland

6th November
1874 Fri: Finished the digging of the rasps today. Took up the dahlia roots. Hoed and cleared the place where they were. Bagra and Ingram taking down ice with the cuddy most of the day. A Ball at Duff House among the Gentry tonight. Proposing a ball among the Artillery tonight. A fine day.

7th November
1874 Sat: I don't mind very well what we was doing today but we cleaned the Walk down from the Bothy to the Fruitroom. Took out some pea stakes etc. A fine day.

8th November
1874 Sun: Slept with Bagra & Munro tonight. At home most of the day. Met in with an old acquaintance as I was going to Church. Went up the length of the Slacks of Tipperty with her. A fine day.

9th November
1874 Mon: Clearing the strawberries the most of the day. Got my Character and my pay from Mr Mackie today as it is the last day I'll be with him. A fine day, slight showers.

10th November
1874 Tue: Left Duff House today at Banff Bridge Station for Edinburgh. Had a long wearisome hurl. Arrived at Edinburgh about 5 o'clock in the evening. Met in with my chum R Ewen at the Station Waverley. Went and got some supper then took a stroll. Met in with some other chaps and had some drink. Then went to bed. Been a fine day but some cold and some showers of snow.

Taking ice with the cuddy – donkey – and necessarily a cart, was an activity that had happened the previous winter too. See note for 15th Dec 1873.

The Ball at Duff House was to celebrate the 25th birthday of Lord Macduff (the future 6th Earl Fife). It had been intended to hold this on his birthday, 10th November, but several of the guests had to leave before then so it was brought forward. "Notwithstanding the short notice, there was a pretty numerous gathering, and the spacious front drawing room of the house had not been so gay for years." Mr Wiseman's band from Aberdeen supplied excellent music, varied occasionally by the performances of Lord Fife's and Lord Macduff's pipers. Refreshments were served in the Vestibule, and the supper room was thrown open at twelve. Dancing was kept up till two."

This photo with many horse drawn carriages at Duff House is a bit later than 1874, but clearly some sort of party was happening!

Slacks of Tipperty – *see note opposite 4th Nov.*

Waverley Station Edinburgh had opened in 1866 (just before this photo), the biggest station in the UK until London Waterloo opening in 1921.

11th November

1874 Wed: Rose about 8 o'clock and had a stroll before breakfast. Got breakfast and then travelled about a while, then we went to D Laird and Laing. Had to stop a good while, there was a great crush but R Ewen went to Thirleston Castle and I came to Vogrie House. We spent the remainder of the day travelling about. then we started the same train for our destination. Arrived at Vogrie all right. Very cold, some showers of snow and it was about an inch over all.

12th November

1874 Thu: The Cook wakened us about half 7 this morning. Commenced to cut down hedges before the Bothy here and working about here at his improvements the whole day. A fine day, cold.

....

Downie Laird and Laing was a large plant nursery in Edinburgh. In particular they had some "Winter Gardens" near to Donaldson's Hospital (no name connection!).

Donaldson's Hospital

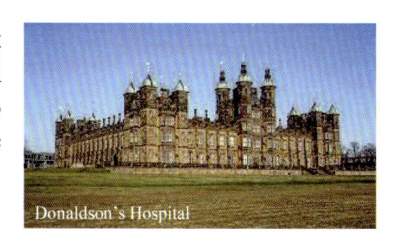

FIG. 135.—NEW WINTER GARDEN AT EDINBURGH.

Such a large and impressive place explains why there were so many people going there, and John and his chum took some time.

For some background to Vogrie House refer to Chapter 2.

CUPHEA.

INDEXES

To demonstrate the number of flowers, fruit and vegetables that were grown at Duff House, indexes for each of these groupings have been made individually.

There is also one for bible references, which John records on most Sundays he attends as the subjects of the sermons. The bible text for these references are given against the relevant date in Chapter 6.

The largest Index is a General Index, including the names and places mentioned throughout the text of this book and the Diary, as well as some general subjects that the Diary mentions (excluding the plants, fruit, vegetables and bible as above).

In these Indexes:

- Where the reference is a date, this refers to a date in the Diary. The Diary dates are 30th Oct 1873 to 12th Nov 1874, so most months can't be confused, but the year is given for good order.

- Where the reference is a number, this refers to the page number in this book (given at the bottom of the page).

- Where a reference is in bold, whether a date or a page number, indicates that there is an explanatory note and/or picture, not just a mention.

Index to Plants	starts at p203
Index to Fruits	starts at p209
Index to Vegetables	starts at p213
Index to Bible references	starts at p219
Index to People, Places and General	starts at p221

The flower images from p200 are contemporary with the time of the Diary, and all of them shown are mentioned therein.

MARIGOLD.

INDEX TO PLANTS (grown at Duff House)

A total of 49 plants are listed within the Diary that John and his fellow gardeners looked after. Most of the list below are flowers; John does sometimes refer to weeding the shrub borders but doesn't name any.

Within this list are also:

- 4 trees, Ash, Holly, Spruce and Willow, only mentioned because they are species he makes use of as part of his job;

- Grass, that he deliberately plants for paths and lawns. This he cuts quite regularly during the summer, using a scythe (the first lawnmower is listed as 1830 but useable designs didn't happen until the 20th century);

- 6 weeds that he spends some considerable effort to remove (Bishop Weed, Chickweed, Clover, Crowfoot, Couch Grass, Dandelions).

Hence there are 39 different plants, mostly flowers, that John has a hand in propagating and looking after. Some of these have several varieties which would add to this total.

The future career he chooses is with flowers, notably Carnations and Lillies; neither of which he mentions while at Duff House!

Name	Action	Date in Diary
Alyssum	Planned	12th Nov 1873
	Planted	11th Mar 1873, 141, 27-28th May 1874
	Potting	6th Oct 1874
Antirrhinum	Took out	12th Nov 1873
Ash	Splitting	17th Feb 1874
Bishop Weed	Forking out	14th Apr 1874
Box (around Horseshoe)	Planted	6-7th Feb 1874
	Preparing edges	6 & 8, 9th Apr 1874
	Laying out	10-11th, 13th Apr 1874
	Taking out old	22nd Apr 1874
	Prepared for new	22nd Apr 1874
	Laying	23rd Apr 1874, 24th Apr 1874
	Cutting	20th Jun 1874
Buttercup		See Crowfoot
Cactus	Shifting	19th Mar 1874
Calceolaria	Planned	12th Nov 1873
	Dug	24th Mar 1874
	Planting	13th Apr 1874, 141, 27-28th May 1874
	Potting	3rd Oct 1874

Cerastium (Snow in Summer)	Planted	11th Nov 1873, 7th Mar 1874
	Took out	12th Nov 1873
Chamomile	Relaying	20th Apr 1874
Chickweed	Hoed	17th Sep 1874
Chrysanthemums	Sent	11th Nov 1873
	Cuttings	25th Mar 1874
Clover	Sowed	28th Apr 1874
Couch grass	Forking out	11th Apr 1874
Crowfoot (buttercup)	Forking out	9-10th Apr 1874
Cuphia	Potting	15th Sep 1874
Dactillis	Planted	11th Nov 1873
Dahlia	Took up the roots	5th Nov 1873
	Tied up in the Vinery	6th Nov 1873
	Took up roots	6th Nov 1874
	Took down	26th Apr 1874
	Planted and staked	30th May 1874
Daisies	Weeding	16th Mar 1874
	Sheeled up	14-16th Apr 1874
	Raked	17th Apr 1874
	Planting	20th Apr 1874
Dandelions	Taking out	14-15th, 18-19th May, 26th Aug 1874

Ferns	Shifting	18th Mar 1874
Fuchsia	Potting	17th Mar 1874
Gasinia	Planted	10th Mar 1874
	Taking out of pots	3rd Apr 1874
Geranium	Shifting	19th Mar 1874
	Planted	30th May 1874
	Potting	14th Sep 1874
	Into greenhouses	29th Oct 1874
Geranium, Bijou	Shifting	17th Mar 1874
	Cuttings	17th Apr 1874
	Cuttings	9th Sep 1874
Geranium, Little Davy	Shifting	16th Mar 1874
Geranium, Stella	Shifting	17th Mar 1874
Geranium, Tom Thumb	Cuttings	12th Sep 1874
Geranium, Trentham Rose	Took out	12th Nov 1873
	Shifting	16th Mar 1874
	Cuttings	12th Sep 1874
Gladioli	Took out the roots	5th Nov 1873
	Put back the roots	22nd Dec 1873
	Planted out	16th May 1874
	Staking	2nd Jul 1874
Grass	Preparing	25th Apr 1874
	Sowed	27th Apr 1874
Ground Elder		See Bishop Weed

Helicrisum	Sowed	14th Apr 1874
Heliotrope	Potting	15th Sep 1874
Holly	Cut	20th, 24th, 25th, 29th Dec 1873
Jonquilla	Planned Planted	12th Nov 1873 27-28th May 1874
Linicia	Planted	10th Mar 1874
Marigold, African	Planned Planted	12th Nov 1873 141, 27-28th May 1874
Marigolds	Sowed	14th Apr 1874
Mignonette	Sowed around Dahlia	**5th May 1874**
Nasturium, dwarf	Planned Planted	12th Nov 1873 141, 27-28th May 1874
Pansies	Potting	15th Sep 1874
Penstemon	Planted Planned Planting	11th, 12th Nov 1873 12th Nov 1873 13th Apr, 141, 27-28th May 1874
Phloxes	Planted Dug Staking	10th Nov 1873 24th Apr 1874 2nd Jul 1874
Pyrethrum	Took up	2nd Feb 1874
Roses	Pruning	2nd Feb, 31st Mar 1874

	Digging and cleaning	28-29th Apr 1874
Salvia	Planted	10th Mar 1874
Salvia, Blue	Planted	12th Nov 1873
Senecio	Potting	15th Sep, 3rd, 6th Oct 1874
Snowdrops	Planted Sent away	29th Nov 1873 30th Mar 1874
Spruce	Cover tender plants	12th Feb 1874
Sweet Williams	Planting	31st Aug 1874
Verbena	Took out Spliced cuttings Potting Planting Potting	12th Nov 1873 25th Nov 1873 9-10th Mar 1874 3rd Apr 1874 14-15th Sep 1874
Viola	Potting	15th Sep 1874
Willow	Taking out the old root Cutting (for baskets)	29th Nov 1873 10th, 16th Dec 1873, 15th Jan, 27th Oct 1874

INDEX TO FRUIT (grown at Duff House)

A total of 14 different types of fruit were grown. This excludes all the different varieties of apples, pears, plums and especially gooseberries, that are mentioned in the Diary, as well as all the different varieties that John doesn't name.

One of the largest activities was producing grapes. A full list of all the actions is included in the Notes against the Diary entries – see page 193 – and is not repeated in this Index. The owner of the major Vineyard of the time noted that 1873-74 seemed to be the peak of the boom time, so Duff House – having had their vines delivered in 1872 was just ahead of their time! Duff House had of course already been growing vines at The Orchard, but from John's Diary in 1874 it seems that those did not ripen as early as the New Vinery grapes had won prizes at the Banff Show (11th Sep) before the first grapes were cut at The Orchard (14th Oct). No doubt this validated the decision to have the New Vinery built.

Some fruits were grown in each of the two gardens. Apricots were only at the Flower Garden, and it seems most of the blackcurrants were either in the Kitchen Garden or Canal Park. Pears grew against the south wall of the Flower Garden because they were already there when the garden was developed in the 1860s, but there were also some in The Orchard.

Fruit	Action	Date
Apple	Taken from store	26th Mar 1874
	Grafted	22nd Apr 1874
	Sent down wind blown	3rd Aug 1874
	Harvested	26th Aug, 1st, 12th, 14th, 23rd, 30th Sep 1874
Apple, Codlin	Harvested	**27th Aug**, 5th Sep 1874,
Apple, Egg	Harvested	**15th Sep 1874**
Apple, Hawthorden		**14th Sep 1874**
Apple, Strawberry Pippins	Harvested	2nd Sep 1874, **179**
Apricots	Clearing space for	2nd Feb 1874
	Got trees	25th Feb 1874
	Planted	28th Feb 1874
	Nailing	2nd Mar 1874
	Covered	11th Mar 1874
	Tied and pinched	17th Jul 1874
Blackberries	Harvested	16th Jul 1874
Blackcurrants	Pruning	26-28th Nov 1873, 20th Jan 1874
	Weeding	3rd Dec 1873
	Harvested	22nd, 23rd, 25th, 27-30th, 31st Jul, 4th Aug 1874
Cherry	Dunged and dug	2nd May 1874
	Tied and pinched	17th Jul 1874

Currants	Hoe	3rd, 4th Jul 1874,
	Harvested	16th Jul 1874, 13th Aug, 10th Sep 1874
	Hoeing	17th Aug 1874
	Tied	1st Nov 1874
Damsons	Harvested	**25th**, 29-30th Sep
Gooseberries	Weeding	1st, 4th Dec 1873
	Pruning	16th Jan 1874
	Took out	20th Jan 1874
	Planted	28th Feb, 5th Mar 1874
	Description, varieties	4th Mar, **1st Jun 1874**
	Hoeing, raking	22nd May 1874, 1st Jun 1874, 10th Jul 1874
	Harvested	24-25th, 27-29th, 31st Jul, 4-6th, 17th Aug, 10th Sep 1874
	Hoeing	26-27th Aug 1874
Grapes	Detailed actions given:	**193**
Pear	Planted	28th Feb 1874
	Tied and pinched	17th Jul 1874
	Grafted	24th Apr 1874
	Harvested	1st Sep 1874
Pear, Black	Harvested	**2nd Oct 1874**
Pear, Jargonelles	Harvested	**1st Sep 1874**
Plum, Gold	Not shifted	23rd Mar 1874
Plum, Patterson	Not shifted	23rd Mar 1874
Plums	Harvested	23rd Sep 1874

Raspberries	Dug	30th Oct 1873
	Hoeing	1st May, 1st Jun, 21st Sep 1874
	Thinning and tieing	13-14th Jul 1874
	Harvested	2nd Sep 1874
	Pruning and tieing	27th Oct 1874
	Made up blanks	3rd Nov 1874
	Adding compost	4th Nov 1874
	Weeding	5-6th Nov 1874
Redcurrants	Weeding	4th Dec 1873,
	Pruning	19th Jan 1874
	Harvested	1st, 10th, 17th Aug 1874,
Rhubarb	Weeding	5th Dec 1873
Strawberries	Dunged	17th Jan 1874, 19th Jan 1874
	Staked	13th Feb 1874
	Filling in	4th Mar 1874
	Hoeing, raking	1st, 4th, 30th Apr, 1st, 22nd May 1874
	Netting	1st Jul 1874
	Harvested	13-14th Jul 1874
	Took nets off	17th Aug 1874
	Cutting the runners	19-20th Aug 1874
	Raking off the straw	21st, 22nd Aug 1874
	Hoed	23rd Sep 1874
	Planted	22nd Jun, **29th Sep 1874**
	Clearing	9th Nov 1874

INDEX TO VEGETABLES (grown at Duff House)

A total of 27 different types of vegetables were grown in 1873-74 at Duff House. This doesn't include the multiple varieties that would have been in use. John states there were 40 varieties of potato, and no doubt lots of other vegetables too; each of these would be kept separate from the other varieties.
NB we have included tomatoes as a vegetable!

Additionally crops of various vegetables were spread out as much as possible around the year. Several sowings of carrots, different plantings of potatoes, onions, celery and cabbages, all presumably so that Duff House could be supplied with produce over as wide a period as possible.

The Ice House is mentioned many times and clearly use was made of this to provide fruit and vegetables to the House – as well as ice to other Duff family estates.

Vegetable	Action	Date
Artichokes	Dung	11th Dec 1873
	Carting	3rd Jan 1874
	Dug up	9th, 10th Jan 1874
	Eaten	25th Oct 1874
Asparagus	Cut	10th Nov 1873
	Dunged	11th Dec 1873
	Taking off the dung	1st Apr 1874
Beans	Sowed	25th Feb, 25th Mar 1874
Beans, French	Preparing	22nd May 1874
	Sowed	30th May 1874
	Harvested	18th, 24th Aug, 1st, 22nd, 29th Sep 1874
Beet	Sowing	7th May 1874
	Harvested	24th Oct 1874
Broccoi	Sowed	25th Mar 1874
Cabbage	Dunged	15th Dec 1873
	Sowed	31st Mar 1874
	Planted	3rd Mar, 11th Jul 1874
	Hoeing	3rd Jun 1874
	Harvested	18th, 25th Aug, 4th, 18th Sep 1874
	Dug	6th Jun, 19th Sep 1874
	Planted	12th Dec 1873, 10th Jun, 23rd Sep 1874, 2nd, 26th Oct 1874
	Clearing	11th Dec 1873, 25th Feb 1874
Cabbage, Red	Planted	6th Oct 1874

Cabbages, Savoy	Harvested	8th Nov 1873
Carrots	Sowed	25th Mar, 13th Apr, 6-7th May 1874
	Harvested	25th Jul, 1st, 15th, 26th, 28th Aug, 10th, 14th, 21st, 23rd Sep, 24th Oct 1874
Cauliflower	Planted	10th Nov 1873
	Sowed	31st Mar 1874
	Earthing up	2nd Oct 1874
	Planted	18th Apr, 6th Oct 1874
	Pricked out	8th, 23rd Oct 1874
Celery	Levelling ridges	10th Dec 1873
	Dunged	13th Dec 1873
	Dug a brake	24th Feb 1874
	Making up ridges	5th Mar 1874
	Pricked out	23rd May, 9th Oct 1874
	Dunged	2nd Jul 1874
	Earthing up	17th Sep, 10th Oct 1874
Cucumber	Prepared	6th May 1874
Gourds	Planting	5th Jun 1874
Greens	Sowed	31st Mar 1874
Herbs	Dug	2nd May 1874
Horseradish	Dug	5th Feb 1874
Kale	Planted	7th Feb 1874

Leek	Harvested	8th, 9th Dec 1873
	Dunged	16th Dec 1873
	Sowed	25th Mar, 13th Apr 1874
Lettuce	Sowed	31st Mar 1874
Marrows	Preparing hillocks	23rd Feb 1874
	Planted	25th Jun 1874
	Thinned and hoed	26th Sept 1874
Onions	Harvesting	3rd Feb 1873, 5th, 8th, 25th Nov 1873
	Sowed	25th Feb, 26th Mar 1874
	Sooted	23rd Mar 1874
	Boned	25th Mar 1874
	Planted	18th Apr 1874
	Weeding	21st May, 2nd, 3rd, 19th Jun, 3rd, 6-7th Jul, 17th Aug 1874
	Harvested	23rd, 25th, 30th Jul, 10th, 15th, 25-26th, 28th Aug, 14-16th, 21st, 26th, 28th Sep 1874
	Sowed	18th Aug 1874
	Weeding	7th, 8th Oct 1874
	Trenching and dunging	28-29th Oct 1874
Parsnips	Harvested	24th Oct 1874
Peas	Sowed	25th Feb, 25th Mar, 6th May 1874
	Staked	9th May, 22nd Jun 1874
	Hoeing	21st May 1874
	Manuring	23rd Oct 1874

Potatoes	Into the pit	**31st Oct 1873**
	Taken to Duff House	20th Nov, 19th Dec 1873, 25th Feb, 18th Mar, 22nd Apr 1874
	Planting	26-28th, 30th, 31st Mar 1874, 7-9th, 14th, 18th Apr, 9th May 1874
	Raking before shoots show	30th Apr 1874
	Weeding	25-27th May, 2nd, 5th, 8th Jun, 8th Jul, 7th, 25th Aug, 30th Sep 1874
	Earthing up	10th, 13th, 15th, 27th, 30th Jun, 13th, 18th, 21st, 22nd, 24th, 27th, 28th Jul, 15-17th, 21st, 23rd, 29th Sep, 15th, 17th, 24th Oct 1874
	Harvested	3rd, 4th, 8-9th, 14-16th Sep 1874
	Take up seed potatoes	30th Sep, 1st Oct 1874
	Put into pit and cover	3rd Nov 1874, 65
Potato, Early Forties		**15th Oct 1874**
Potato, Prince Regent		**15th Oct 1874**
Spinach	Sowed	25th Mar 1874
	Hoeing and raking	4th Apr 1874
	Hoeing	1st May 1874
	Dunged	29th Jul 1874
Sprouts	Taking up	9th Dec 1873, 5th Feb 1874
	Sowed	31st Mar 1874
	Planted	29th Sep 1874
Tomatoes	Picked	1st Sep 1874
Turnips	Hoeing and raking	4th Apr 1874
	Sowing	30th Apr 1874

Example of a box edged path (similar to some of the beds in the Duff House Flower Garden)

INDEX OF BIBLE REFERENCES

Book	Date in Diary
Acts	4th Jan 1874
Collossians	2nd, 30th Nov 1873
Corinthians	23rd Nov, 21st Dec 1873
Deuteronomy	16th Nov 1873
Hebrews	15th Feb 1874
John	9th, 30th Nov, 7th Dec 1873
Luke	14th Jun, 21st Jun 1874
Malachi	26th Apr 1874
Matthew	14th Dec 1873
Psalms	28th Dec 1873
Timothy	25th Jan 1874
Timothy 2	18th Jan 1874

VERBENA.

SALVIA.

GENERAL INDEX (people, places etc)

John mentions a surprising number of places that he visits during his year of apprentice gardening at Duff House; all these are indexed with the date(s) and where possible a note about each of these places (generally highlighted in bold in this Index).

In trying to explain some of the people and places that John mentions, we have inevitably made reference to many more as well. If these are not mentioned in the Diary itself then the reference in this Index is just a page number (given at the bottom of each page).

Name	Page or date
Adam, William	27, 69
Agnes, Lady	see Hay, Lady Agnes
Airlie Gardens	**Chapter 5B** and multiple entries
Airlie House	53, 54, 55, 56
Airlie, Earls of	53
Albert	1st Jan 1874
Alvah, Bridge of	30, 18th Jan, 1st Mar, 18th Apr, 13th Sep, 18th Oct 1874
Alvah, Church	27th Sep 1874
Ardmiddle	15th Nov 1873, 167
Astoria (Long Island)	14
Astoria Bowling Team	17
Australia	2nd Dec, 3rd Dec 1873, 18th Jun 1874
Bagra, Mr	multiple entries
Ball (at Duff House)	**6th Nov 1874**
Ballindalloch	75
Ban Righ (ship)	131
Banff	**Chapter 3** and multiple entries
Banff Bridge	30, 69
Banff Bridge Station	**157**, 159, 10th Nov 1874
Banff Castle	177
Banff Cemetery	189
Banff Court House	25,
Banff Court House	177
Banff Foundry	137
Banff market	21st Nov 1873
Banff Parish Church	139
Banff Station	11th Nov 1873, **157**, 159
Banff, Lord	53

Banffshire Horticultural Association	177
Bankhead (Macduff)	87
Bannock	18th Feb 1874
Bar of Banff	24
Barclay, John	10th Aug 1874
Barclays	87
Baron Skene (ship)	**18th Apr, 3rd May 1874**
Basket (Cobb)	**109** and multiple entries
Bathing	4th, **6-8th**, 14th, 25th, 28-29th Jun, 5th, 12th, 23rd, 26th Jul, 9th, 16th Aug, 20th Sep 1874
Belle Halliday (Carnation)	14
Bellevue Road	189
Big Gun (Volunteers)	**17th Apr 1874**
Birds, Stuffed	**30th Aug 1874**
Black Bull Inn	105
Blackbirds	**10-11th Mar**, 10-11th Jul 1874
Blyth, William (Blacksmith)	137
Boat	8th, 25th Aug 1874
Boathouse (Duff House)	29, 24th May, 8th Jun 1874,
Boathouse (Lifeboat)	18th Jan 1874
Bobbies	7th Sep 1874
Boswell, James	105
Bothy (Airlie Gardens)	40, 59, 3rd Nov 1873, 1st Feb, 10th Aug, 17th Aug, 1st Nov 1874
Bothy (The Orchard)	40, 6th Oct 1874
Boyndie Road	7th, 10th Jan 1874
Braco's House	36
Bremner, George (Photographer)	89
Brewery (Banff)	**4th Jan**, 99, 4th Oct 1874
Brodie, Alexander (sculptor)	32
Brough, Miss	13th Mar 1874

Bruce, Rev WS (Bruce of Banff)	**30th Oct**, 7th, 14th Dec 1873, 15th Feb, 26th Ap, **14th Jun**, 165, 4th Oct 1874
Bryce (wing, Duff House)	27, 28, 29
Buckie	11th Nov 1873
Bullfinch	29th, **31st Jan 1874**, 113
Burgh Council	45, 60
Burroughs Hyatt, T	14
Caie, Rev WS	10
Canal	6th Dec 1873
Canal Door	8th Nov, 6th, 30th Dec 1873, 7th, 10th Jan, 26th Mar, 4th May 1874
Canal Park	**Chapter 5B.1**
Canal Street Floral Market	15,
Carmelite Monks	175
Carmelite St	139
Carnation, Belle Halliday	14
Carney, Alexander (ropeworks)	87
Cat	17th Aug 1874
Catholic Chapel (Banff)	**29th Mar**, 20th Sep 1874,
CDV	31st Dec 1873, **26th Mar**, 187, 5th Nov 1874
Chalmers, John (Spirit Dealer)	89
Changing of the Hours	17th Nov 1873, 23rd Feb 1874
Charlotte (ship)	113
Chelsea (Veitch)	12
Chimney	24th May 1874
Clark, John	13th Mar 1874
Clayton, Dr	20th Dec 1873
Cleland, Mr	4th Nov 1873
Cleland, Mrs & family	7th Nov 1873
Clerk, John (engraver)	56
Clock, Old Church	**16th May 1874**

Clovenfolds	79, 193
Coal	99, 8th Apr, 135, 14th Aug, 6th Sep 1874
Cockburn, Miss	26th Mar 1874
Cockers (Nurserymen)	**4th Nov 1874**
Colleonard Nurseries	97
Collie Lodge	21, 23
Commercial Bank of Scotland	177
Connoisseur	173
Conversation Lozenges	**4th Dec 1873**
Cordiner	56
Court House (Banff)	25
Cow	3rd, 4th Apr 1874
Craig, Margaret	153
Craig, William	29th Nov, 7th Dec 1873, 14th Jun, **29th Jun 1874**
Cricket	24th Jun 1874
Crow Wood	**5th**, 18th Apr 1874
Cuddy (Donkey)	**15th Dec 1873**, 6th Nov 1874
Culloden, Battle	35, 55
Cumberland, Duke of	55
Cureton, Thomas	18
Czar (of Russia)	101
D, Miss	16th, 18th Nov 1873
D, Miss	17th Mar 1874
Davidson, Miss	3rd Aug 1874
Dawson, John (Blacksmith)	137
Deer Park	**3rd Apr 1874**
Delgatie Castle	31
Deveron Valley	151
Deveron, River	multiple entries
Dewar, James (Vogrie House)	11
Disraeli	107
Donadson's Hospital (Edinburgh)	199

Donaldson, Alexander (son)	17
Donaldson, Ethel (daughter)	17
Donaldson, George (father)	10
Donaldson, Isabella	17, 7th Apr 1874
Donaldson, James (brother)	10, 1st Feb 1874
Donaldson, Jane (wife)	17
Donaldson, Jessie (mother)	10
Donaldson, Jessie (sister)	10
Donaldson, John	**Chapter 2** and multiple entries
Doocot	**56**, 57
Downie, Jane	18th Feb 1874
Downie, Laird and Laing	**11th Nov 1874**
Drill Hall	See volunteers
Duff House	**Chapter 4** and multiple entries, **6th Nov 1874**
Duff House Park	2nd Aug 1874
Duff House, looking round	23rd, 30th Aug, 4th Nov 1874
Duff, Alexander (1st Earl's father)	53
Duff, Alexander (Viscount Macduff)	**Chapter 4**
Duff, family tree	31
Duff, James (2nd Earl)	181
Duff, James (5th Earl)	**Chapter 4** and multiple entries, **6th Jul**, 31st Oct 1874
Duff, James Cunnigham Grant	171
Duff, Lady Agnes Cecil Emmeline	32
Duff, Lady Alexina	32
Duff, Lady Anne Elizabeth Clementine	32
Duff, Lady Ida Louise Alice	32
Duff, Sir William Robert	107
Duff, William (1st Earl Fife)	53, 55
Duncan (cartographer)	36

Duncan (gamekeeper)	2nd Apr, 2nd, 29th Sep, 29th Oct 1874
Duncan, Honourable Hamilton	97
Duncan, John	81
Dunfermline	17
Easter	125
Eden	9th, **22nd Aug**, 20th, 26-27th Sep, 17th, 22nd, 25th Oct 1874
Edinburgh	10th Nov 1874
Edinburgh, Duke of	23rd Jan 1874
Edward, Thomas	103
Election	12th Feb 1874
Elgin	18th Jun 1874
Elmhurst (Long Island)	14
Emmett, Susannah	81
Episcopalean Church Rectory	75
Essex (ship)	99
Essie Ann (ship)	169
Ewen, Jane(t)	115
Ewen, Miss (Ann?)	23rd Dec 1873
Ewen, Robert	4th Mar, 10th, 11th Nov 1874
Faed, James (artist)	67
Fast Day	**2nd Apr**, 22nd Oct 1874
Father	4th Jan, 10th, 27th Feb, see also 7th Apr 1874
Ferguson, Rev (author)	65
Feu de joie	23rd Jan 1874
Fife Arms Hotel	51, 4th Dec 1873, **105,** 16th, 19th, 30th Sep 1874
Fife, Earl, Duke & Duchess	8, **Chapter 4,** 45, 22nd Nov 1873
Findlater, Lord	36
Findlay, Alexander (Potatoes)	189

Fisher's Gate	30
Fishing	25th, 29th Aug 1874
Fleming, George	71
Flower Garden (Airlie Gardens)	**Chapter 5B** and multiple entries
Fochabers	19-20th Jul 1874
Fordyce	30th Oct 1873
Foresters	18th Jan 1874
Forglen House	167
Forglen School	10
Fraser, John (Blacksmith)	137
Fruitroom	59, 3rd, 22nd Nov, 23rd Dec 1873, 12th, 23rd Feb, 23rd Mar, 20th Apr, 29th Jul, 7th, 19th Oct, 7th Nov 1874
Funkieston	191
Gallowhill	22nd Aug, **17th Oct 1874**
Gamekeeper	2nd, 22nd Apr, 2nd, 29th Sep, 29th Oct 1874
Gamekeepers Cottage	85
Gamrie	See Gardenstown
Garden-Campbell, Mr	187
Gardenstown	17, 16th Nov 1873, **90,** 8th Feb 1874
Gaveney Brae	**15th Mar 1874**, see also 147
Geddie, John and William	131
Gentles, Thomas	23
Gerrard, John and James (Cartwrights)	6th Sep 1874
Gladstone	107
Gleaston Castle	173
Goldsworth (Head Gamekeeper)	22nd Apr, 29th Sep 1874
Gordon Castle	**2nd Jan,** 25th Mar, 19th, **20th July 1874**
Gordon-Lennox, Angus & Zara (Gordon Castle)	161

Goukstanes	97
Grant, Rev James (Fordyce)	77
Gray, Laing (Blacksmith)	137
Gray, Miss (Hannah?)	21st Dec 1873
Greenbanks	23rd Jan 1874, 131, 191
Gun	15th Nov 1873
Gushet corner	3rd Dec 1873
Hampers	11th Nov 1873
Hardy, John	25th Mar 1874
Hardy, Mr	7th, 11th Nov 1873, 11th, 13th Jul 1874
Hawk	24th, 28th Feb, 8th Mar 1874
Hay, Lady Agnes (wife of 5th Earl)	31, 57
Hay, William (painter)	56
Head Gardener's House	**44**, **81**
Henry, Jane (wife)	17
Herb Border	8th Nov 1873,
Herring Boats	14th Aug 1874, 191
Hill of Down	**13th Jan 1874**,
Hillhead of Mountblairy	9,
Horseshoe	Chapter 5 and multiple entries
Hospital Island	73, 85
Hunter, Rev William (Macduff)	75
Hurley	**19th Dec 1873**
Hurricane	**21st Oct 1874**
Ice	19th, 23rd, 29th Dec 1873, 13th Jan, 6th Nov 1874
Ice House	36, 3-8th Nov, 15th Dec 1873, 12-14th, 19th Feb, **111**, 30th Oct 1874
Imlach, James	55, 173

Ingram	25th, 27th, 28th Dec 1873, 19th Feb, 7th, 25th, 26th Mar, 3rd, 4th Apr, 7th May 1874
Innes House	31, 34, 8th Nov, 11th, 15th, 23rd Dec 1873, **91**
Innes, William	19th Dec 1873
Inverness	165
Iran	119
Jacobite	35, 55
Jock	6th Sep 1874
Johnson, Samuel	105
King Edward	22nd Oct 1874
King, Gen James Stewart	159
King's Ford	30
Kingshorn	6th Jan 1874
Kinnaird, Mrs M & Mr (Spirit Dealer)	89, 95
Kippin, Old	8th Jun 1874
Kirkside	30, 25th Jul 1874
Kitchen Gardens	**Chapter 5B.2**
Landowners in Banffshire	133
Laundry	12th, 15th Feb 1874
Lawson, Peter and Sons	77
Lemon, Mr	30th Aug 1874
Lesmurdie	**19th Jul 1874**
Lifeboat	**99**
Lillies	14
Lime	23rd Mar, 13th Apr 1874
Links (Banff)	1st Jan 1874
Llanbryde	91
Llanbryde Parish School	34
Lodging of Airlie	see Airlie House

Long Island	14
Longmores (Merchants)	**30th Apr 1874**
Losan	1st Sep 1874
Loughcrew Gardens	119
Louise, Princess	34
Low, Joseph and Ellen (Chemist)	17
Lyons	15th Nov 1873
Macduff	19, 113, 19th Apr, 3rd May, 1st Aug, 26th Sep 1874
Macduff Church	75, 30th Nov 1873
Macduff Harbour	14th Aug 1874, 169
Macduff Station	**157**, 159
Macduff, Marquess	34
Macduff, Viscount	**Chapter 4**, 10th Nov 1873, 12th Feb, 2nd, 6th Nov 1874
Mackie, James (Spirit Dealer)	89
Mackie, Mr (Head Gardener)	multiple entries
Mahood	58
Mahood (Author)	175
Maraces	11th Mar 1874
Market (Banff)	21st Nov 1873, 22nd May 1874
Marr Lodge	173
Marsden, William (Spirit Dealer)	89
Mary (coffee pot)	18th Dec 1873
Maundy Thursday	125
Mausoleum	36, 67, 73
McBean, James	18th Jun 1874
McKenzie, Christina (aunt)	10
McKenzie, Janet (grandmother)	10
McKenzie, Jessie (mother maiden)	10
McPherson Grant, Sir George and Lady	75, 131
McPherson, G	18th Apr 1874

M'Donald, Miss	135
Melvin	2nd, 3rd Jan 1874
Melvine, J	16th, 30th Mar, 1st, 25th Apr, 20th May, 20th Sep, 16th Oct, 5th Nov 1874
Mill	26th Dec 1873, **2nd Apr 1874**,
Milne, Mr	8th Dec 1873
Milne, Mrs (Ardmiddle)	73
Mitchell	2nd, 19th Apr, 10th May, 11th, 23rd, 25th, 30th Aug, 13th Sep 1874
Mohr church	73, **90**
Moles	12th May, 21st Jun 1874
Montcoffer	18th Jan, 12th, 17th Feb, **181**, 25th Oct 1874
Moody and Sankey	**2nd Aug 1874**
Mountblairy, Hillhead of	9
Mungo	24th Sep 1874
Munro	8th Nov 1874
Murray, Andrew (Spirit Dealer)	89
Murray's Institution (Macduff)	165
Muscat	13th Jan 1874
Music Hall, Aberdeen	179
Mutton Bells (Macduff)	26th Sep 1874
Myatt, Joseph	29th Sep 1874
Netherbrae	12th Apr 1874
Netherwood	**22nd Oct 1874**
New Road	47
New Year Festivities	93
New York	17
New York Flower Exchange	15, 16, 17, 18
Newmill	159
Nissen huts	30

Nurses Home	55
Ocean Queen (ship)	169
Ogilvie	55
Ogilvy	53, 55
Orchard	**Chapter 5A** and multiple entries
Owl	28th Feb 1874
Pall Mall, London	31
Palm House	58, 59
Parkinson, John (Author)	179
Patchogue	18
Pathhead (Vogrie)	11, 163
Peel, Robert	177
Pennell, Elizabeth Robins	19
Persia	119
Photographers	10th Oct 1874
Picnic	29th Jul 1874
Pig	4th Dec 1873, 8th Jan 1874
Pineapple	3rd Dec 1873
Pipers	197
Pirie, Mr	5th Nov 1873
Plantation	17th Jan 1874
Police, Banffshire Constabulary	177
Portessie	169
Portknoockie	135
Portsoy	99
Primary School, Banff	23
Princess Louise	34
Pyper	11th, 18th Jan, 15th Feb, 2nd, 11th Apr, 9th Aug, 20th Sep 1874
R, Miss	28th Dec 1873, 4th Jan 1874

Rabbits	29th Sep, 11th Oct 1874
Rae and Son (Photographer)	89
Raeburns	24th Nov 1873, **77**, 4th Apr 1874
Regents Park	13,
Registrar	27th Feb 1874
Reid, William (Blacksmith)	137
Reidhaven, Lord	12th Feb 1874
Ribbon	71, **141**
Richmond & Gordon, Duke of	133
Robinson, George	95
Ropeyard	25th Dec 1873
Rose, William	181
Roy, General - map	30, **35**
Royal Oak	25th Dec 1873
Russian Muscat	13th Jan 1874
Sanders, John	173
Sandyhill Road	5th Apr 1874
Sankey, and Moody	**2nd Aug 1874**
Scotland, Mr (Commercial Bank)	177
Scury Island	30, 85
Scythe	7th May, 17th Aug, 22nd Sep 1874
Seafield, Earl of	107
Sean	25th Dec 1873
Sellar, Lewis	1st Apr 1874
Shah Nasser al-Din	119
Shand, Mr	11th Nov 1873
Shearer	17th Feb 1874
Show, Aberdeen	18th Sep 1874
Show, Alvah	21st Jul 1874, 163
Show, Banff	3rd Mar, **11th Sep 1874**, 185
Show, Fyvie	**13th Aug 1874**
Show, Turriff	**11th Aug 1874**

Sim, Mary	85
Simpsons (Jeweller)	23rd Jun, 2nd Jul 1874
Sinclair, Mr	177
Skene Duff, Hon George	181
Slacks of Tipperty	**195**, 8th Nov 1874
Smith	2nd Apr, 20th, 27th Sep, 25th Oct 1874
Smith, Alex	16th Aug 1874
Smith, Miss	7th Nov 1873
Smithy	**7th May**, 17th Aug 1874
Soot	23rd Mar 1874
Souter, John Bulloch	65
Souvenir of Sympathy	81
Spade, The	27th, 29th Dec 1873
Squirrel	1st Mar, 5th Apr, 1st Nov 1874
St Bridget's Nurseries	12,
St Mary's Chapel	73
St Mary's Well	14th Nov 1873
Starlings	24th May 1874
Statues, lead	54
Stephen, Miss	17th, 20th Mar, 11th Oct, 5th Nov 1874
Stonehaven	113
Straw	19th Feb, 21st Aug, 12th Oct 1874
Sutherland, Duke and Duchess	71
Talia	69
Tampa	18
Tarlair	9th Aug 1874
Tayler, Mr & Mrs of Glenbarry	75
Tennant family (Innes House)	91
Term Day	26th May 1874
Terry's of York	79
Theatrum Botanicum	179

Thirlestane	11th Nov 1874
Thomson, William	79, 193
Thorpe, Dr	11th Nov 1873
Thrashing Mill	3rd Sep 1874
Tipperty, Slacks of	**195,** 8th Nov 1874
Town and County Club	95
Trentham	71
Troup	28th Dec 1873, 7th, 8th Feb, 9th May, 20th Jun, 25th Jul, 13th, 29th Aug, 19th Sep, **10-11th Oct,** 1st Nov 1874
Trousers	2nd, 5th Oct 1874
Trust House	105
Turners	13th Jan 1874
Turriff	22nd Oct 1874
Turriff Bridge (covered)	69
Tweed Vineyards	**3rd Dec 1873, 26th Oct 1874,** 193
Union Square Flower Market	15, 16
Urquhart	91
Veitch Nurseries	11,
Veitch, Harry James	12,
Venus, Temple of	55, 97
Vinery (at Airlie Gardens)	**Chapter 5B.3**
Vinery (at The Orchard)	**Chapter 5A**
Vogrie House	**11,** 11th Nov 1874
Volunteers	46, 27th, 30th Dec 1873, **89,** 1st, 23rd Jan, **17th,** 29th Apr, 18th May, 19th, 25th Jul, 6th Nov 1874
Volunteers Hall	See Volunteers

Walker, Jessie (Royal Oak)	87
Wardine	18th Feb 1874
Warren Clouston, Mrs K	173
Watch	23rd Jun, 2nd Jul 1874
Waterhens	21st Dec 1873
Watson, William	99
Watt, James (Spirit Dealer)	89
Waverley Station, Edinburgh	**10th Nov 1874**
Webster	16th Aug 1874
Webster, James	1st Feb 1874
Webster, John (Gordon Castle)	161
Westfield Farm, Inverkeithing	10,
Whin Hill	See Gallowhill
Williams	15th Nov 1873
Williamson, Robert (Farmer)	191
Wilson, William	14
Wilsons Institution	23
Winter Gardens	199
Wiseman, little	15th Feb 1874
Wiseman, Mr	16th Nov 1873, 11th, 18th Jan, 15th Feb, 2nd Apr 1874
Wiseman, Mr (Band)	197
Wood, Frank (Brewery, Banff)	99
Wood, John (Cartographer)	42, 57
Woodland Walk	153
Wrack Woods	67, 77
Wrights	11th Oct 1874
Zoological Gardens (Regents Park)	13

SCARLET GERANIUM.